ITALIAN COOKING

Ruth Bauder Kershner

WEATHERVANE
BOOKS

contents

introduction to italian cooking

Italian cuisine is as hearty and varied as the Italian landscape, extending from the sunny Italian islands to the mountains north of Turin and the Piedmont. Italy is composed historically of many small city-states which have for centuries vied with each other for supremacy in all things from the arts to the food they eat. Geographically, Italy is not easily traversed. It is divided by the Appenine mountains and other smaller ranges. Many areas are quite isolated and have developed their own regional cuisine. For these reasons, there is no one true, easily described Italian cuisine but rather a wide spectrum of delicious dishes of many different origins and influences. Many of the dishes mentioned here are cooked throughout Italy but are given a special touch or flair in each area to make them unique. Italian cuisine is based predominantly on the indigenous products of the many regions. Foods are relished at the peak of freshness, very often with little embellishment. The emphasis is on the true, natural flavor of the food.

Italian cuisine is also historically rich, stemming from the time of the Romans, with some of the dishes still a part of the cuisine today. For example, polenta is served in the north of Italy today. It stems from early Roman times when polmentum, a thick grain porridge was served as a staple of the diet. Today, cornmeal or farina is used, but the product is similar in texture. Many of the fruits and vegetables were introduced into the diet in ancient times. Cabbage and fava beans were grown and eaten. Spinach was introduced by the Saracens in the 9th century A.D. A variety of fruits were grown and many imported from far-away parts of the Roman empire. Apricots, apples, peaches, cherries, figs and melons were all cultivated. After the fall of the Roman empire, the cultivation of these crops continued to be refined.

By the late 13th century, pasta had been discovered by an inventive Italian cook and such notations were found in ancient cookbooks. Contrary to popular theory, Marco Polo did not bring pasta from China. Marco Polo did, however, establish a thriving spice trade with the Far East and helped make Venice rich. During the Renaissance, Italy continued to refine her cuisine. Cooking schools sprang up in Florence and cuisine was considered a fine art. A true marriage of cuisines resulted from the marriage of Catherine D'Medici to King Henry II of France. Catherine brought to Paris with her some of the finest cooks of the court of Florence. The French were introduced to fine delicate pastries, desserts and many new vegetables. French cuisine of the period was much less refined in character. Thus, the Italian cuisine can be considered the ''Mother Cuisine'' of the classic French cookery. The Venetians brought coffee to Italy from the Arab countries in the late 15th century and it has remained an important part of the Italian way of life.

Some of the foods that we consider important aspects of Italian cookery were not introduced into Italy until after Colombus had discovered the New World. Tomatoes, then only small golden orbs, were introduced in Italy in the mid-16th century. Through careful cultivation, today Italy boasts large, red ripe tomatoes, that form the basis for the thick red sauces of Southern Italy. Red peppers, corn, potatoes, kidney beans and turkey were also imported from the New World and assimilated into the Italian cuisine.

Italian cuisine today is robust and varied and its dishes can now be found all over the world. Pasta is of course a staple of Italian cuisine. Spaghetti and macaroni are popular in the south of Italy and frequently served with a variety of sauces. Noodles and other flat pasta products are served in the north and are frequently made at home. Butter is the primary fat used in cooking in the north of Italy. Dairy cattle are prominent in that region and butter is easily obtained. In the south of Italy, the mountainous, more populated land will not support large herds of cattle. Olive trees have, for centuries, thrived in this area and the subtle flavor of olive oil permeates the food. Veal, beef, lamb, delicious cured hams, sausages, and pork are eaten throughout the country. With an extended seacoast, Italian cuisine features many delicious fish dishes, prepared in all of the seacoast towns and villages. Game is eaten in the mountainous regions where hunting is an integral part of the way of life. Fresh fruits and vegetables are grown wherever possible. In a country where refrigeration is still not ubiquitous, shopping daily for food is still common. Fresh fruit and vegetables are eaten at their peak with a very short lag between the garden and the table. Poultry and eggs are prepared in a thousand delicious ways. Cheese, in the warm southern climate, is especially important since it is an important way of using fresh milk. Crisp, crusty bread accompanies most meals and may be made at home or purchased depending on the region. Fresh food can indeed be considered one of Italy's natural resources. The Italian people savor their food and enjoy eating with an almost reverential respect. Meals are a time for the family to be together and holidays and celebrations center around food.

A word should be said here about the Italian way of eating, which is continental in character. Breakfast is light, usually consisting of coffee with milk or tea or chocolate with bread and jam. Coffee is often taken at mid-morning. In Italian cities, there are many coffee bars. They are relaxed places where business is often transacted over coffee and a snack of pastries or sandwiches. The main meal of the day is usually eaten about one o'clock. It can be an elaborate meal consisting of many courses and requiring several hours to eat, or more simple for everyday meals. The meal usually begins with an antipasto. It can consist simply of a few relishes or fresh melon and country-cured ham or it can be quite elaborate with a wide choice of meats, cheeses and relishes. Minestra is the second course and may consist of a hearty soup, pasta with sauce or rissotto. Next meat, fish, or poultry is served accompanied by vegetables or salad. Bread and wine are served throughout the meal. Coffee follows the meal. Pastries are served usually on holidays. Fresh fruits and delicious table cheese are by far the most popular finale for a large meal. After the meal, a well earned afternoon rest is usually taken. In the late afternoon, strolling is a common pastime. The ladies enjoy coffee and pastries or the delicious gelati, a rich ice cream. The men relax over an aperitif. Italy is known for several renowned aperitifs, namely, vermouth and Campari. Supper is a lighter meal, usually eaten at seven in the evening or later, and often features a hearty soup.

This book contains a variety of recipes from both the north and south of Italy. Thanks to some very generous friends and relatives, there are some delicious family recipes included here. Italian cuisine is infinitely adaptable. It is equally delicious for an elaborate party or an everyday family dinner. We hope that you will find a variety of delicious and satisfying dishes included here. Happy cooking and delicious eating!!

a word about ingredients

Most of the ingredients necessary for fine Italian cooking are available at your local grocery store. Select the freshest possible ingredients, of the highest quality, making substitutions only when absolutely necessary. You may find a trip to a local Italian grocer or delicatessen well worth your while for obtaining the best of ingredients. The following notes may help you in the selection of ingredients:

Oil: Olive oil is a basic ingredient in most Southern Italian recipes. Select a good quality imported or domestic olive oil, as it adds a subtle flavor. If you must, substitute any mild flavored vegetable oil, for example soy, cottonseed or safflower oil.

Cheese: Cheese is a staple of the Italian diet. Summarized here are a few of the basic cheeses used in cooking.

Ricotta: This is a fresh cheese that is soft and creamy in texture and mild in flavor. Buy it fresh at the grocery or Italian market or if unavailable substitute small curd cottage cheese, pot cheese or farmer cheese.

Mozzarella: This is a bland white cheese that melts easily. It may be made from whole or partly skimmed milk. It is widely available in supermarkets. Jack or Meunster cheese might be substituted if Mozzarella is unavailable.

Parmesan and Romano: These are hard grating cheeses. If you possibly can, buy a well-aged piece of cheese and grate it when you are ready to use it. Already grated Parmesan and Romano cheeses, purchased at the market, generally lack flavor. Store the cheese tightly covered in the refrigerator.

Fontina: This cheese is creamy in color and melts easily. It has a distinctive taste all its own that some say is like truffles. If Fontina cheese is unavailable, try substituting a well-aged Swiss or Emmenthaler cheese.

Pasta: Pasta is the back bone of the Italian diet. It is the collective name applied to any of over 500 varieties of spaghetti, noodles, macaroni and like products, made from flour, water and sometimes eggs. There are two basic classes of pasta: Flat noodles and tubular macaronis. Flat noodles are more commonly used in the North of Italy where they are frequently made at home. Homemade pasta is indeed delicious and well worth the effort. Tubular macaronis have for centuries been made in factories in the south of Italy. They come in a myriad of sizes and shapes that range from tiny to enormous tubes and intricate shapes such as seashells, spirals, thin and thick spaghettis, wheels, and much more. In a simple recipe calling for cooked pasta topped with sauce, the various macaronis may be used interchangeably. Be sure to read the directions carefully on the package and cook in plenty of boiling salted water until done. Cooking time will vary with the type, quality, and quantity of pasta cooked. A small amount of oil may be floated on the surface of the cooking water to help keep the pasta from sticking. Drain and serve immediately, tossed with the sauce. Domestic or imported pasta may be used. Many imported pastas are made with semolina and are less starchy than domestic pasta. Test several brands and shapes to decide what your family likes best.

Herbs and spices: Herbs and spices are widely used in Italian cookery. Any well stocked spice shelf will generally meet all of your needs. Oregano, sweet basil, garlic and flat leaf parsley are frequently used in Italian cookery. Of course, the fresher the herbs the better. In Italy, they are picked from the garden.

Wines: The national beverage of Italy is wine. From the youngest to the oldest Italian, wine is universally enjoyed especially with meals. Every district has its own special wines and many local wines with no particular name are of good quality. Among the more famous red wines are: Chianti Classico, Bardolino, Valpolicella, Red Barolo and Barbera. Many superb white wines are also available: Soave Bolla, Orvieto and Frascati to name a few. Consult your local wine dealer to find out what is available in your area, at a price you can afford. Many domestic wines are available, of good quality and imitate the classic Italian wines well. For cooking, use a domestic wine in the moderate price range.

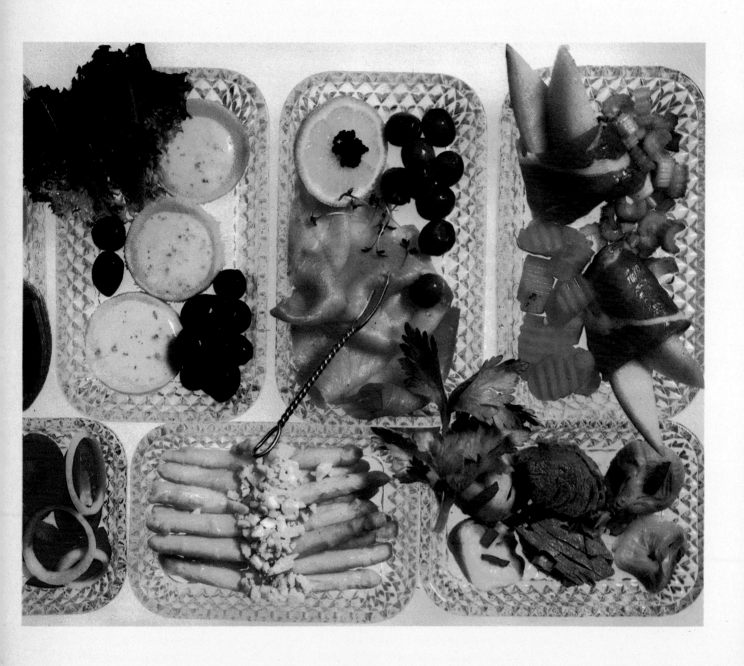

cold antipasto tray

antipasto

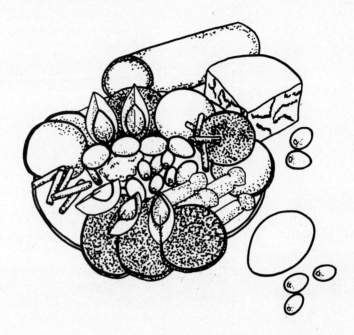

antipasto

Antipasto literally translated means before the meal. It is usually an assortment of cold appetizers, artfully arranged and garnished. Generally, it is a selection of cold meats and cheeses and a few pickles and vegetables. However, one or two hot items add variety, especially for a special meal or party. A selection of antipasto ingredients, plus a few hot appetizers, could compose a complete light, buffet meal on a warm summer night or be served at a cocktail party.

An eighth pound of assorted meats and cheeses accompanied by several small portions of vegetable appetizers would generously serve one person. If hot appetizers or a large meal is planned, keep the antipasto small. Bread or bread sticks and an aperitif or a glass of wine make good accompaniments.

Below is a short list of possible ingredients from which to choose. The variety of ingredients is by no means limited to those on this list! Use your imagination and the ingredients you have on hand. Visit an Italian grocer or delicatessen and try several meats and cheeses as well as the pickled vegetables, olives and other items available.

Select one or several ingredients from each group:

Meat: Capocollo, Mortadella, Proscuitto, salami, pepperoni

Cheese: Mozzarella, Provolone, Caciocavallo

Fish: Oil-packed tuna (select the best grade available and an Italian brand if possible) garnished with capers, sardines, anchovies

Vegetables: Carrots, celery, cherry tomatoes, pearl onions, artichoke bottoms filled with tarragon-flavored mayonnaise, asparagus spears marinated in Italian dressing and garnished with a chopped hard-cooked egg, green olives, ripe olives, black salt-cured olives

Commercially available products: Caponata (an eggplant relish from Sicily) served with toasted Italian bread, or melba toast, pickled mushrooms, marinated artichoke hearts, gardinera (assorted vegetables pickled in vinegar), pepperonata (hot pickled peppers)

The recipes that follow in this chapter can be served as a part of an antipasto assortment or served alone as a smaller first course. These recipes may also double as sides dishes in many cases. Consider using the recipes in the fish and main course chapters in the same manner. For example, tiny hot meatballs or small portions of scampi make excellent appetizers.

melon with prosciutto
melone con prosciutto

½ of a large ripe honeydew or
    cantaloupe
¼ pound prosciutto
A pepper mill

Remove the seeds and rind from the melon and slice into crescents. Cut the ham slices in half and wrap a piece of ham around each piece of melon. Arrange on a platter and grind fresh pepper over the ham and melon just before serving.

Lemon or lime wedges are a suitable garnish. Makes 4 to 6 servings, depending on the number of other appetizers.

Note: Fresh ripe figs or papaya may be substituted for the melon.

marinated garbanzo beans
ceci con oregano

2 16-ounce cans garbanzo
    (ceci) beans
½ teaspoon salt
¼ teaspoon freshly ground
    pepper
½ teaspoon dried oregano,
    crumbled
¼ cup olive oil
Finely chopped parsley

Drain the garbanzo beans well. Place in a serving dish. Add the salt, pepper, oregano and oil and stir well. Garnish with parsley and refrigerate several hours before serving.

Makes 6 servings.

Note: White beans (cannelli beans) or kidney beans can be substituted for the garbanzo beans. One 4-ounce can of drained, oil-packed tuna may also be added if cannelli beans are used. Hard-cooked eggs, peeled and sliced, and quartered tomatoes would make a tasty garnish.

stuffed olives
olive imbottite

1 6-ounce can jumbo pitted
    black olives
1 2-ounce can anchovy fillets
2 tablespoons olive oil
1 clove garlic, minced
2 tablespoons finely chopped
    parsley
12 stemmed cherry tomatoes
½ of a medium green pepper,
    thinly sliced

Drain the olives. Drain the anchovy fillets and cut each one in half. Stuff each olive with ½ of an anchovy fillet. Place in a serving bowl. Combine the olive oil, garlic and parsley and pour over the olives. Mix well. Chill several hours. Bring to room temperature before serving.

Garnish with the cherry tomatoes and green peppers. Be sure to provide cocktail picks for your guests to spear these nibbles.

Makes 6 servings.

eggs stuffed with tuna
uova al tonno

6 hard-cooked eggs, peeled
1 4-ounce can oil-packed tuna, drained
1 tablespoon minced parsley
½ tablespoon capers, finely chopped
1 tablespoon mayonnaise
½ teaspoon garlic powder
¼ teaspoon freshly ground black pepper
Parsley
Pimiento slivers

Cut the eggs in half lengthwise and remove the yolks. Put the yolks in a small bowl and mash with a fork. Drain and finely chop the tuna. Add to the egg yolks along with the parsley, capers, mayonnaise, garlic powder, and pepper. Mix very well and stuff the egg whites with the yolk and tuna mixture and garnish with parsley and pimiento. Chill well.

Makes 6 servings as a part of an antipasto platter.

crab balls
granchie arancini

1 pound crab meat
4 tablespoons butter, or margarine
1 teaspoon salt
⅛ teaspoon cayenne pepper
1 teaspoon dry mustard
1 teaspoon dehydrated parsley flakes
2 teaspoons Worcestershire sauce
½ cup soft bread crumbs
2 egg yolks, lightly beaten
½ cup flour
Oil for frying

Pick over the crab meat and remove any bits of shell and cartilage. Flake the crab meat and place in a mixing bowl. Melt the butter or margarine in a small saucepan. Add the seasonings and bread crumb mixture and egg yolks to the crab and mix well. Refrigerate for 2 to 3 hours or until stiff enough to be handled easily. Form into 35 small balls the size of a walnut. Dredge in flour. Heat several inches of oil in a heavy saucepan or deep-fat fryer to 360°F. Fry the crab balls until golden brown and serve hot.

Garnish with parsley and lemon wedges.

Makes 35 balls.

clams casino
vongole alla casino

2 dozen cherrystone clams
2 tablespoons olive oil
1 tablespoon butter
½ cup finely minced onion
¼ cup finely chopped green pepper
2 cloves garlic, peeled and chopped
1 cup dry bread crumbs
4 slices crisp bacon, crumbled
½ teaspoon dried oregano, crumbled
2 tablespoons grated Parmesan cheese
Parsley flakes and paprika
Olive oil

Wash and scrub the clams well to remove the grit. Place on a baking sheet and place in a 450°F oven until the shells open. Remove the meat from the shell and chop. Reserve the chopped clams and discard ½ of the shells. Heat the oil and butter in a small skillet. Add the onion, pepper and garlic and sauté until tender. Remove from the heat and cool. Add the bread crumbs, bacon, oregano, Parmesan cheese, and the reserved clams and mix well. Fill the clam shells with the mixture. Sprinkle with the parsley flakes and paprika and drizzle with olive oil. Bake in a 450°F oven until lightly browned (about 7 minutes). Serve hot.

Makes 6 servings.

stuffed artichokes
carciofi imbottiti

4 medium-sized globe
   artichokes
¾ cup dry bread crumbs
3 tablespoons grated
   Parmesan cheese
1 tablespoon chopped parsley
½ teaspoon garlic salt
¼ teaspoon dried oregano,
   crumbled
¼ teaspoon pepper
2 tablespoons butter
2 tablespoons olive oil
1 cup boiling water

Remove the stems from the artichokes. Cut about ½ inch from the tips of the leaves with a pair of kitchen shears. Drop into boiling salted water and cook 5 minutes. Drain and shake to remove the water and cool.

Combine the bread crumbs, cheese, parsley, garlic salt, oregano and pepper and mix well. Tap the base of the artichokes on a flat surface to spread the leaves. Stuff each artichoke with ¼ of the bread crumb mixture, spooning it between the leaves. Place the artichokes in a saucepan or stove-top casserole, placing them close together so that they do not tip over. Top each artichoke with ½ tablespoon of butter and ½ tablespoon of oil. Pour the boiling water into the dish or pan. Cover and cook over low heat 35 to 45 minutes or until the artichokes are tender.

Makes 4 servings.

stuffed mushrooms I
funghi ripieni I

1 pound medium or large
   mushrooms
1 cup dry bread crumbs
2 tablespoons dried parsley
   flakes
2 tablespoons grated
   Parmesan cheese
¼ teaspoon garlic powder
Salt and pepper
5 tablespoons olive oil, divided

sauce
1 small onion, chopped
2 teaspoons olive oil
1 8-ounce can tomato sauce
½ teaspoon sugar
¼ teaspoon oregano,
   crumbled
¼ teaspoon garlic powder
Salt and pepper

Wash the mushrooms well and remove the stems. Hollow out the mushroom caps slightly by scraping with a teaspoon. Drain well and pat dry. Combine the bread crumbs, parsley, Parmesan cheese, garlic powder, salt and pepper and 2 tablespoons olive oil and mix well. Fill the mushrooms with the crumb mixture. Pour 3 tablespoons of olive oil in the bottom of a shallow baking dish. Tilt to coat the dish evenly. Place the mushroom caps in the oiled baking dish.

Next prepare the sauce. Sauté the onion in the oil in a small pan until tender. Add the remaining ingredients, stir well and simmer 10 minutes. Pour the sauce evenly over the mushrooms. Bake at 350°F for 30 minutes.

Makes 4 servings.

stuffed mushrooms II
funghi ripeni II

1 pound large mushrooms
1 pound bulk sausage
Salt and pepper
¼ teaspoon garlic powder
2 eggs
¼ cup grated Parmesan
   cheese
¾ cup Italian-style bread
   crumbs
¼ cup olive oil

Wash the mushrooms and pat dry. Stem the mushrooms and hollow the caps slightly with a spoon. Chop the stems. Brown the sausage and mushroom stems in a heavy skillet. Drain well. Remove from the heat and cool. Add the salt and pepper and garlic powder. Beat the eggs and cheese together and add to sausage mixture along with the bread crumbs and mix well. Pour the oil into a 13 × 9 × 2 inch baking dish and tilt to coat. Dip the outside of the mushroom caps in the oil and turn to coat. Stuff with the sausage mixture and place side by side in the baking dish. Bake at 375°F for 20 minutes. Serve hot.

Makes 4 to 6 servings, depending on how many other antipasto dishes you are serving.

italian vegetable dip
bagna cauda

italian vegetable dip

½ cup olive oil
½ cup butter
4 garlic cloves, peeled and
   finely minced
1 2-ounce can anchovies,
   drained and finely chopped
Freshly ground pepper
10 to 12 cups assorted raw
   vegetables, peeled, trimmed
   and cut-up: cherry
   tomatoes, green peppers,
   celery, carrots, mushrooms,
   cauliflower, radishes, and
   zucchini
1 loaf crusty Italian bread, cut
   into slices

Heat the butter and olive oil together over low heat in a fondue pot or a ceramic bagna cauda pot (or heat in a skillet and pour into a casserole with a candle warmer). Heat gently so that the butter does not brown. Add the garlic and anchovies and continue to cook until the anchovies dissolve and the mixture is bubbly. Reduce the heat so that the mixture stays warm but does not brown and serve with the vegetables and bread. Provide your guests with forks so that they can spear the vegetables, swirl in the sauce, and eat holding the bread like a napkin under the vegetables to collect the delicious drippings.

Makes 6 servings.

mozzarella cheese sandwiches with anchovy sauce

mozzarella en carrozza

anchovy sauce

¼ cup butter
2 anchovy fillets
1 tablespoon drained capers, chopped
2 tablespoons chopped parsley
Juice of ½ lemon

mozzarella cheese sandwiches

16 thin slices of Italian bread (½ inch thick)
8 thick slices mozzarella cheese (⅜ inch thick)
3 eggs
Salt to taste
½ cup dry bread crumbs
¼ cup butter or margarine

First, prepare the anchovy sauce. Melt the butter in a small skillet. Do not brown. Under cold running water, rinse the anchovies. Chop finely and add with the capers and parsley to the butter. Add the lemon juice and stir well. Keep warm.

Remove the crust from the bread. Lay one slice of cheese between two slices of bread and press together. In a small bowl beat the eggs and a pinch of salt. Dip the bread and cheese sandwiches in the egg and dredge in the bread crumbs. Heat the butter or margarine over moderate heat in a heavy skillet. Add the cheese sandwiches and cook until golden brown on one side and turn and cook on the other side.

Serve immediately topped with the anchovy sauce.

Makes 8 3-inch sandwiches (4 servings).

mozzarella cheese sandwiches with anchovy sauce

soups and salads

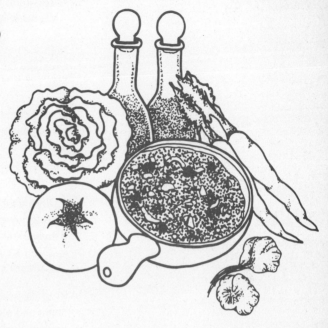

split pea soup
zuppa di piselli

2 cups split peas
Water
1 large onion, finely chopped
  (about 1½ cups)
1 clove garlic, peeled and
  minced
1 ounce salt pork, chopped
3 tablespoons olive oil
1½ cups tomato sauce
1 teaspoon sugar
Salt and pepper
1 bay leaf
1 cup uncooked small shell
  macaroni
Grated Romano cheese

Pick over the split peas and rinse well. Place in a small bowl and cover with water. Soak overnight. In a large saucepan, sauté the onion, garlic and salt pork in the olive oil until the onion is tender. Add the soaked peas, water to cover the peas, the tomato sauce, sugar, salt and pepper and bay leaf. Simmer, covered, over low heat 1½ to 2 hours or until the peas are tender. Remove the bay leaf and add the macaroni and additional water if the soup is too thick. Cover and simmer for 20 minutes.

Serve hot, sprinkled with the grated Romano cheese.

Makes 4 to 5 servings.

tomato–rice soup
zuppa di pomodoro e risi

2 tablespoons butter
½ cup chopped onion
½ cup chopped celery
1 28-ounce can peeled tomatoes
1½ cups chicken broth
½ teaspoon dried marjoram, crumbled
½ teaspoon dried sweet basil, crumbled
2 teaspoons sugar
Salt and pepper
⅓ cup long-grain rice
Grated Parmesan cheese

Melt the butter in a large saucepan. Sauté the onion and celery until limp. Combine the tomatoes, chicken broth, and the onions and celery and butter in a blender jar and blend until smooth. Pour back into the saucepan. Add the marjoram, sweet basil, sugar, and salt and pepper to taste. Bring the mixture to a boil over moderate heat. Add the rice, stir well and cover. Reduce the heat to low, and simmer 15 to 20 minutes or until the rice is tender. Serve garnished with Parmesan cheese.

Makes 4 servings.

pavian soup
zuppa pavese

4 slices white bread
3 tablespoons melted butter
5 cups chicken stock *or* 2 13-ounce cans regular strength chicken broth
4 eggs
6 tablespoons shredded Parmesan cheese

Trim the crusts from the bread. Brush on both sides with the melted butter and place on a cookie sheet. Bake at 350°F for 30 minutes, or until golden. Pour the stock into a large shallow saucepan and heat to boiling. Reduce the heat to low, then break the eggs one at a time into a saucer and slide into the liquid. Poach lightly. Remove with a slotted spoon and keep warm. Strain the stock, return to the pan and heat to boiling. Put one toasted bread slice in each soup bowl. Top with 1 poached egg. Ladle the soup over the egg.

Sprinkle each bowl with 1½ tablespoons of cheese and serve.

Makes 4 servings.

pavian soup

green soup with meatballs

zuppa verde con polpette

½ pound fresh spinach or beet greens
½ cup water
¼ teaspoon salt

soup

¾ pound lean ground beef
½ cup dry bread crumbs
¼ cup grated Parmesan cheese
1 egg, well beaten
½ cup parsley, finely chopped
Salt
White pepper
4 cups beef broth (homemade or canned)

Remove the stems from the spinach and rinse well. In a medium saucepan, heat the water and salt. Add the spinach, reduce the heat to low and cook for 3 minutes. Drain well and coarsely chop.

In a bowl combine the ground beef, bread crumbs, Parmesan cheese, egg, parsley, salt and pepper. Mix well and form into walnut-sized meatballs. In a large saucepan, heat the beef broth to boiling. Add the spinach and meatballs and bring to a boil again. Reduce the heat to low, cover and simmer 15 minutes and serve.

Makes 4 servings.

stuffed stewed chicken

zuppa di pollo imbottiti

This makes a beautiful 2 course dinner in a pot!!

stuffing

2 tablespoons butter
1 chicken liver
½ cup chopped onion
1 cup ground ham
½ cup chopped fresh parsley
½ pound hamburger
1 egg
¼ cup dry bread crumbs
2 tablespoons grated Parmesan cheese
¼ teaspoon ground nutmeg
Salt and pepper

soup

1 3-pound chicken
8 cups water
2 carrots, peeled and sliced
2 celery stalks, sliced
1 onion, sliced
½ cup chopped fresh parsley
1 turnip, peeled and diced
1 bay leaf
½ teaspoon thyme
Salt and pepper
Paprika

First prepare the stuffing. Melt the butter in a small skillet and sauté the chicken liver and onion until the onion is lightly browned and the liver is cooked through. Add the onion and pan drippings to the remainder of the stuffing ingredients in a mixing bowl. Chop the chicken liver finely and add to the stuffing. Mix well.

Wash the chicken well and pat dry. Pack the stuffing into the chicken cavity and truss the openings shut. Tie the legs together and tie or pin the wings next to the body. Place the chicken in a large deep kettle (a Dutch oven will do). Add the water, vegetables and seasonings and bring to a boil. Reduce the heat to low, skim any foam from the surface of the water. Cover and simmer 2 hours or until the chicken is well done.

Remove the chicken from the pan and keep warm. Skim the fat from the broth. Add cooked noodles or rice if you wish and serve as a first course. Then, carve the chicken and serve the chicken and stuffing accompanied by rice or potatoes and the vegetables of your choice as the main course.

Makes 4 servings.

sicilian sausage soup

zuppa di salsiccia alla siciliana

¼ pound sweet Italian sausage (with the casing removed)
½ cup finely chopped onion
¼ cup chopped peeled carrots
¼ cup chopped celery
2 tablespoons chopped parsley
1 16-ounce can Italian-style peeled tomatoes, broken up with a fork
1 13¾-ounce can regular strength chicken broth
½ teaspoon dried sweet basil, crumbled
¼ cup orzo (rice-shaped macaroni for soup, also called "soupettes")
Salt and pepper

In a medium skillet, brown the sausage, breaking it up in small pieces as it cooks. Remove from the skillet with a slotted spoon and place in a large saucepan. Sauté the onion in the sausage drippings until tender. Remove the onion with a slotted spoon and add to the sausage. Add the vegetables, chicken broth, and sweet basil to the sausage mixture. Bring the soup to a boil and stir well. Cook over moderate heat for 15 minutes. Stir in the orzo and salt and pepper to taste. Reduce the heat to low and simmer covered for 20 minutes or until the orzo is tender.

Makes 4 servings.

chicken broth with filled pasta

capelletti en brodo

pasta
1 recipe Egg Noodles (see Index)

filling
¾ cup ricotta cheese
¼ cup grated Parmesan cheese
2 tablespoons chopped parlsey
Salt and white pepper, to taste

soup
3 10¾-ounce cans condensed chicken broth
3 soup-cans water

or

8 cups homemade chicken stock

First make the pasta according to the recipe. Cover with plastic wrap and let stand 30 minutes. Meanwhile make the filling. In a small mixing bowl, thoroughly mix the ricotta and Parmesan cheese, parsley and salt and pepper to taste.

On a lightly floured surface, roll the dough ¼ at a time, until paper thin, keeping the remainder of the dough tightly covered. If using a pasta machine, roll to slightly less than 1/16th of an inch. Cut into 2-inch rounds with a floured biscuit cutter. Reroll the scraps. To fill, top each round with ¼ teaspoon of the filling. Dampen the edge of the circle with a little water and fold into a half-moon shape. Place the filled pasta on a plate or tray and cover until all are completed.

For the soup, combine the chicken broth and water in a large saucepan and bring to a boil over moderate heat. Add the filled pasta and cook for 5 to 10 minutes or until tender. Ladle into soup bowls and serve with grated cheese.

Cappelletti can be made in advance and frozen (uncooked) in a single layer on a cookie sheet. Transfer to a freezer bag and keep frozen until ready to cook. Frozen pasta will require slightly longer to cook.

Makes 8 servings (90 to 100 filled pasta if rolled by machine).

Note: To adjust this recipe for more or fewer servings, allow 1 cup of broth per person and 10 to 12 capelletti.

quick minestrone
minestrone rapido

soup
6 cups trimmed cut-up
  assorted fresh vegetables
  selected from the following
  list: broccoli, cauliflower,
  green beans, swiss chard,
  spinach, peas, and celery
6 tablespoons butter or
  margarine
2 tablespoons olive oil
6 cups beef stock or canned
  beef broth
Salt and pepper

garnish
3 tablespoons olive oil
1 clove garlic, peeled
2 cups diced stale Italian
  bread
Grated Parmesan cheese

In a large kettle or Dutch oven, sauté the vegetables in the butter and olive oil until they begin to soften. Add the beef stock or broth and salt and pepper to taste. Cook over high heat for 20 minutes or until the vegetables are tender.

Meanwhile, prepare the garnish. Heat the oil in a small skillet with the garlic clove until the garlic is browned. Discard. Sauté the bread in the oil over moderate heat until golden. Serve the soup garnished with the bread cubes. Pass the Parmesan cheese.

Makes 5 to 6 servings.

neopolitan minestrone
minestra napoletana

1½ pounds beef shanks
1 onion, quartered
1 package soup greens (or 2
  celery stalks, 1 carrot, 1
  potato, 1 turnip and a sprig
  of parsley, all cleaned and
  chopped)
1 small bay leaf
2 whole peppercorns
1 clove

1½ teaspoons salt
6 cups water
1 celery root
¼ pound ham
2 ounces penne or elbow
  macaroni
3 tablespoons tomato paste
1 teaspoon dry chervil
4 tablespoons grated
  Parmesan cheese

In a large Dutch oven, combine the beef shanks, onion, soup greens, bay leaf, peppercorns, clove, and salt. Add the water and bring to a boil. Skim any foam. Reduce the heat to low and simmer covered 1½ to 2 hours. Remove the meat and cool. Strain the broth and skim the fat. Return the broth to the pot. Clean the celery root and cut into thin sticks. Dice the meat from the beef shanks and cut the ham into thin strips.

Boil the macaroni until tender in boiling salted water and drain. Bring the broth to a boil. Combine the tomato paste with 1 cup of the broth and stir until dissolved. Add to the broth in the pot along with the celery root, diced beef and the ham. Cover and cook 15 minutes. Add the macaroni and chervil and heat through.

Sprinkle with the Parmesan cheese and serve.

Makes 6 servings.

minestrone roman style

minestrone alla romano

3 strips bacon or ham fat
2 large onions, coarsely
  chopped
2 cloves garlic, peeled
½ teaspoon salt
1 16-ounce can red kidney
  beans
6 cups beef stock or broth
  (Use Beef Stock recipe here
  or any other beef stock or
  broth)
⅓ cup olive oil
2 medium potatoes, peeled
  and diced
2 small carrots, peeled and
  sliced
1 medium zucchini, trimmed
  and sliced ½ inch thick
½ cup sliced celery
1 16-ounce can peeled
  tomatoes
1 teaspoon dried sweet basil,
  crumbled
1 cup finely shredded cabbage
1 cup chopped cooked beef
  (optional)
¼ cup uncooked pastina
½ cup red wine
Salt and pepper
Grated Parmesan cheese

Render the bacon or ham fat in a large deep kettle. Remove the cooked bacon or cracklings. Sauté the chopped onions in the bacon fat until lightly browned. Mash the garlic cloves with the salt and add to the onion mixture.

Add the beans and their liquid and the beef broth to the kettle. Bring to a boil. Reduce the heat to low and cook covered for 30 minutes.

Meanwhile, heat the olive oil in a large, heavy skillet. Add the potatoes, carrots, zucchini and celery and cook over moderate heat, stirring occasionally, for 10 minutes.

Add the vegetable mixture to the soup pot. Add the tomatoes and sweet basil and stir well. Simmer 15 minutes. Add the shredded cabbage, cooked beef, pastina and wine and cook for 20 to 30 minutes. Taste for seasonings and add salt and pepper to taste. Serve with freshly grated Parmesan cheese.

Makes 6 servings.

beef stock

3 pounds beef shank and neck bones

2 medium onions, coarsely chopped

4 carrots, peeled and chopped

3 stalks celery (with the leaves), chopped

1 turnip, peeled and chopped

¼ cup chopped parsley

1 tablespoon salt

10 cups water

Preheat the oven to 375°F. Place the beef bones in a shallow metal roasting pan and bake, turning occasionally, until well-browned. Transfer the bones and the fat and juices to a large (16-cup) kettle. Add the remaining ingredients and simmer for 3 hours. Refrigerate. Skim, remove the bones and reserve any meat clinging to the bones. Strain the broth. Taste for seasoning. If the broth seems bland, add several teaspoons of instant broth granules. Freeze any leftovers for future use.

tomato salad with basil dressing

insalata pomodori con basilico

dressing
½ cup olive oil
3 tablespoons red wine vinegar
1 teaspoon dried sweet basil, crumbled
½ teaspoon garlic salt
Freshly ground pepper

salad
1 head romaine lettuce
3 medium tomatoes, peeled and thickly sliced
1 medium onion, peeled and sliced
1 8-ounce ball mozzarella cheese

Combine the dressing ingredients in a screwtop jar or bottle and shake well. Clean the romaine and place on a serving platter. Arrange overlapping slices of tomato, mozzarella, and onion on the platter. Refrigerate until serving time. Then, shake the dressing well. Pour over the salad. Serve immediately.

Makes 4 servings.

green salad with croutons

insalata verde

croutons
1 clove garlic, peeled and sliced
1 cup cubed stale Italian bread, with the crust removed (save for bread crumbs)
2 tablespoons olive oil

salad
1 medium head iceberg lettuce
1 medium head romaine lettuce or endive
¼ cup grated Parmesan cheese

dressing
½ cup olive oil
¼ cup red wine vinegar
½ teaspoon dried oregano, crumbled
½ teaspoon salt
¼ teaspoon pepper

First, prepare the croutons. Heat the olive oil in a small skillet and sauté the garlic in the oil over moderate heat until lightly browned. Remove the garlic with a slotted spoon and discard. Add the bread cubes and sauté, stirring frequently, until golden brown. Drain on paper towels.

Combine the dressing ingredients in a bottle or screw-top jar and shake well. Allow to stand at room temperature. Clean the lettuce and pat dry. Tear into bite-size pieces and place in a salad bowl. Refrigerate until serving time.

To serve, sprinkle the salad with the cheese and croutons. Shake the dressing well and pour over the salad.

Toss well and serve immediately.

Makes 4 to 6 servings.

pepper and tomato salad

insalata pepperoni e pomodori

2 medium green peppers
3 medium firm ripe tomatoes
½ cup olive oil
2 tablespoons red wine vinegar
½ teaspoon dried sweet basil, crumbled
1 tablespoon dehydrated parsley flakes
Salt and pepper, to taste

Clean the green pepper and cut in thin lengthwise slices. Core the tomatoes and cut into thin slices. Arrange in a serving dish. Combine the olive oil, vinegar and seasoning and combine well. Pour over the vegetables and refrigerate several hours before serving.

Serves 4 or 5.

cold macaroni and bean salad

insalata di maccheroni e fagioli

2 cups cooked, drained macaroni
1 16-ounce can red kidney beans, drained
1 medium green pepper, cleaned and chopped
½ cup finely chopped onion
½ cup finely chopped celery
¼ cup salad oil
¼ cup wine vinegar

1 clove garlic, minced
½ teaspoon dried sweet basil, crumbled
½ teaspoon dried oregano, crumbled
Salt and pepper
¾ cup mayonnaise
Green pepper rings
Sliced hard-cooked eggs

In a bowl, combine the macaroni, beans and vegetables, mixing well. Combine the salad oil, vinegar, garlic, sweet basil, oregano, salt and pepper and mix well. Pour the dressing over the salad and mix well. Refrigerate, covered, for several hours. Add the mayonnaise and mix well. Garnish with the green pepper rings and hard-cooked egg slices.

Makes 6 servings.

cold potato and beet salad

insalata di patate e barbabietole

2 fresh beets
2 medium potatoes
½ cup chopped green onion
¼ cup olive oil
3 tablespoons wine vinegar

1 teaspoon dried sweet basil, crumbled
½ teaspoon dry mustard
Salt and pepper
1 head Boston lettuce, cleaned

Do not remove the stalks from the beets. Just wrap them well in aluminum foil. Wash the potatoes and prick with a fork. Preheat the oven to 450°F. Bake the beets for 1 hour. Place the potatoes in the oven and continue baking 1 hour more. Remove the beets and potatoes from the oven and allow to cool.

Remove the skins from the beets and potatoes and cut into ½-inch-thick slices. Combine the beets, potatoes, and onions and mix gently. Combine the olive oil, wine vinegar, sweet basil, mustard, salt and pepper and mix well. Pour over the beets and potatoes and mix gently. Refrigerate for several hours, covered, to mellow the flavors.

Serve at room temperature in a bowl garnished with the Boston lettuce. Makes 4 servings.

neopolitan minestrone

cauliflower salad
insalata di cauliflore

1 small head cauliflower
¼ cup chopped red pepper or pimiento
2 tablespoons chopped fresh parsley (Italian flat leaf if available)

¼ cup sliced black olives
1 tablespoon capers, chopped
1 tablespoon wine vinegar
3 tablespoons olive oil
½ teaspoon dried oregano, crumbled

Wash the cauliflower, clean it and separate into flowerettes. Slice the flowerettes into thick slices. Cook in boiling salted water until crisp, but tender.

Drain well. Gently mix the cauliflower, pepper, parsley, olives and capers in a serving bowl. Combine the wine vinegar, olive oil and oregano and mix well. Pour over the salad and refrigerate 1 hour before serving.

This salad may be garnished with anchovies if you wish. Makes 4 servings.

Note: Other cooked vegetables — for example, beets, broccoli or green beans — may be substituted in this recipe.

green salad with croutons

semolina dumplings—roman-style

pepper and tomato salad

sauces, pasta, rice and other grain dishes

egg noodles— charcoal makers style
tagliatelle alla carbonarra

2 tablespoons olive oil
¼ pound lean, thick sliced
  bacon
A pinch crushed, dried red
  pepper flakes
2 tablespoons butter
3 quarts water

3 teaspoons salt
1 tablespoon cooking oil
12 ounces tagliatelle or broad
  egg noodles
3 medium eggs, well beaten
½ cup freshly grated
  Parmesan cheese

In a heavy skillet, heat the olive oil. Chop the bacon and fry in the oil until crisp. Add the pepper flakes and butter and heat just until the butter melts. Remove from the heat.

Meanwhile, bring the 3 quarts of water to a boil. Add the salt and oil. Add the noodles and cook until they are al dente (tender, but still firm in texture). Drain. Add immediately to the bacon mixture. Pour the eggs over the noodles and toss the eggs, bacon and noodles together. The mixture should be hot enough to "cook" the eggs. If the eggs do not appear cooked, continue to toss the noodles over very low heat for 1 or 2 minutes.

Makes 3 to 4 servings.

egg noodles
*pasta fresca
all'uovo*

1⅓ cups flour
½ teaspoon salt
2 eggs
2 teaspoons olive oil
2 teaspoons water

Combine the flour and salt in a mixing bowl. Make a well in the center. Beat the eggs, oil and water together and pour into the well. Mix thoroughly, adding a little more water if necessary to form a stiff dough. Turn out on a lightly floured surface and knead to form a smooth, elastic dough (about 15 minutes). Let rest, covered, for 30 minutes.

To roll by hand: Divide the dough into 4 equal parts. Lightly flour a smooth surface and roll the dough ¼ at a time until it is as thin as you can roll it. Ideally it should be 1/16th of an inch thick. Select a ball-bearing rolling pin if possible, since it is very easy to get blisters. Cut according to the recipe of your choice or use the following to substitute for package noodles:

Tagliatelle: Roll up like a scroll and cut into ⅜ inch strips. Unroll and dry on a towel.

Lasagne: Cut into strips 2 inches wide and as long as your baking dish. Dry on towels.

Manicotti: Cut into squares 5 × 5 inches and dry on towels.

To roll by pasta machine: If you enjoy homemade noodles and pasta and make them frequently, a pasta machine might be a good investment for you. It consists of two rollers that can be moved close together or far apart and and turned by a crank. Several cutting blades are also provided. The machine can also be used to roll wonton wrappers or certain specialty breads such as poppadums. It is not necessary to knead the dough by hand if you are rolling the dough by machine as both operations can be accomplished at the same time.

Let the dough rest without kneading and then divide into quarters. Take the dough, one-quarter at a time, and pass the dough through the machine with the rollers set as far apart as possible (usually number 10 or the highest numerical setting on the machine). Fold the dough into thirds and pass through again. After passing the dough through the machine 10 times, turn the setting down one notch and roll through. Continue to roll the dough, reducing the setting one notch each time, until the desired thickness is achieved. The dough strip will become long. Do not fold it. If it becomes unwieldy, cut it in half and roll the pieces separately. Roll to slightly less than 1/16th of an inch thick. Cut as directed above, and dry.

Noodles can be prepared ahead. Simply roll them, cut, and dry for ½ hour and then freeze. It is best to quick-freeze the noodles on a tray and then carefully transfer them to a bag or box and seal. Remove from the freezer when ready to use and cook the same as you would freshly made pasta.

To cook, bring 4 to 5 quarts of salted water to a boil. Float 1 tablespoon of oil on the surface of the water. Add the pasta a few pieces at a time and stir. Cook until the pasta floats to the surface of the water. Test for doneness. It should be firm, and not mushy. Drain well.

Makes about ¾ of a pound. The yield for the pasta recipes given is based on machine-rolled pasta. If you are rolling the dough by hand, make twice the amount of dough, since the product will not be as thin. If you have extra, make noodles and freeze them for future use.

Variation: To make green noodles, omit the water and add ¼ cup of well-drained, cooked and pureed spinach and proceed as above.

semolina dumplings— roman style
gnocchi alla romana

2 cups milk
1 tablespoon butter
½ teaspoon salt
A pinch of freshly grated
  nutmeg
Ground white pepper, to taste
½ cup farina (or semolina)
2 eggs, beaten
½ cup grated Parmesan
  cheese

for garnish
2 tablespoons melted butter
1 tablespoon grated Parmesan
  cheese

Butter a cookie sheet and set aside. In a heavy saucepan, combine the milk, butter, salt, nutmeg, and pepper and bring to a boil over moderate heat. Slowly add the farina, stirring constantly. Reduce the heat to low and cook until very thick and a spoon will stand unsupported in the center of the pan. Remove from the heat. Add the eggs and Parmesan cheese and mix well. Spread on the cookie sheet in a rectangle ½ inch thick. Refrigerate until firm.

Cut into rounds about 1½ inches in diameter (or cut into squares or triangles, if you prefer). Arrange in a greased casserole or baking dish, slightly overlapping. Drizzle with the melted butter and sprinkle with the Parmesan cheese. Bake in a preheated 350°F oven for 20 minutes. Serve hot.

Makes 3 to 4 servings.

cornmeal pudding
polenta

½ cup coarse yellow cornmeal
2 cups water (divided)
¾ teaspoon salt
2 tablespoons butter or
  margarine
¼ cup freshly grated
  Parmesan cheese

topping
3 tablespoons butter
2 tablespoons freshly grated
  Parmesan cheese

Combine the cornmeal with ½ cup of cold water, stirring well. In a medium saucepan, combine 1½ cups cold water and the salt and bring to a boil. Slowly stir the cornmeal mixture into the boiling water, stirring constantly to prevent lumps. Cook over medium heat, stirring occasionally until very thick (approximately 25 to 30 minutes). Remove from the heat and stir in the 2 tablespoons of butter and ¼ cup of cheese.

Pour the mixture into a 4 × 8-inch or other small loaf pan and chill one hour. Turn out on a wooden board and slice ¾ inch thick. Place the slices, overlapping, in a small casserole. In a small skillet, heat the remaining 3 tablespoons of butter until lightly browned. Pour over the polenta and sprinkle with the remaining cheese. Bake in a 350°F preheated oven for 20 minutes. Broil 1 to 2 minutes, until the cheese is bubbly and the top lightly browned.

Alternately, the polenta may be served freshly cooked from the saucepan topped with gravy, marinara sauce, or your favorite tomato sauce and cheese.

Makes 4 servings.

venetian rice and peas
risi-bisi

3 tablespoons butter or
  margarine
¼ cup chopped onion
2 cups regular-strength
  chicken broth
1 cup raw long-grain rice

1 10-ounce package frozen
  green peas
½ cup cooked ham, diced
Salt and pepper
Grated Parmesan cheese

In a large saucepan, melt the butter and sauté the onion until transparent. Meanwhile, heat the chicken broth to boiling. Add the rice to the onions and stir to coat with the butter. Add the peas, ham, and chicken broth and stir well. Cover and cook over low heat approximately 20 minutes or until all of the liquid is absorbed.

Sprinkle with Parmesan cheese and serve.

Makes 4 to 6 servings.

rice, milanese-style
rissotto alla milanese

½ small onion, finely minced
½ cup long-grain white rice
1 tablespoon butter
1 tablespoon olive oil
2 teaspoons beef marrow
2 tablespoons dry white wine

Pinch of saffron
2 cups hot beef broth
1 tablespoon butter
2 tablespoons grated
  Parmesan cheese

Sauté the onions and rice in the butter and olive oil over moderate heat until very lightly browned. Add the beef marrow and cook gently until it melts. Add the wine and cook until it is absorbed. Dissolve the saffron in the hot beef broth.

Add the beef broth a little at a time and continue to cook, stirring constantly, until all of the liquid is absorbed and the rice is tender and creamy in consistency. This process should take 18 to 20 minutes. Stir in the remaining butter and the Parmesan cheese and allow the cheese to melt. Serve immediately. Rissotto does not reheat well.

Makes 4 servings.

My sister-in-law Charlotte's mother prepares this northern Italian dish for her family. As Charlotte warned me when I first prepared this dish, don't be put off by the appearance, because it is simply delicious!!

saucepan stuffing
panna

3 cups water
½ teaspoon salt
2¾ cups dry bread crumbs
  (plain or Italian-style)

1 egg, lightly beaten
Salt and pepper
2 tablespoons butter
Grated Parmesan cheese

In a medium saucepan, combine the water and salt and bring to a boil. Slowly add the bread crumbs while stirring constantly. Stir well so that there are no lumps. Reduce the heat to low. Cover the pan and cook for 1 hour, stirring occasionally. Remove from the heat and cool slightly. Add the egg and stir well. Add salt and pepper to taste and the butter and return to the heat for 10 more minutes, stirring constantly to keep the mixture from sticking. Turn into a serving dish, sprinkle with Parmesan cheese and serve. Makes 4 servings.

Note: Italian-style (seasoned) bread crumbs used for all the bread crumbs in this dish is too strong for many people's taste. My family prefers half Italian-style bread crumbs and half plain bread crumbs for a milder flavor.

macaroni with sauce amatrice

penne con salsa amatrice

sauce

2 tablespoons olive oil
2 cloves garlic, peeled and minced
¼ pound salt pork, diced
1 small onion, chopped
¼ cup dry white wine
1 28-ounce can Italian plum tomatoes, drained and minced
1 teaspoon sugar
1 teaspoon chili powder
½ teaspoon paprika
½ teaspoon dried sweet basil, crumbled
½ teaspoon dried oregano, crumbled
Salt and peper

pasta

3 quarts water
1 tablespoon salt
1 tablespoon cooking oil
12 ounces penne or other macaroni
Grated Parmesan cheese

Heat the olive oil in a large saucepan. Add the garlic, salt pork, and onion and sauté until the onion is tender. Add the white wine and cook until it has evaporated. Add the tomatoes and spices and simmer 20 minutes, uncovered.

Meanwhile, heat the water to boiling. Add the salt and float the oil on the surface of the water. Add the penne and cook until al dente. Drain. Place in a serving bowl, top with the sauce and serve with Parmesan cheese.

Makes 4 servings.

macaroni with sauce amatrice

fettuccine with butter and cheese
fettuccine al burro

1 recipe Egg Noodles
  (see Index)
½ cup butter, cut in small
  pieces

1 cup freshly grated Parmesan
  cheese
Freshly ground black pepper

Prepare the noodle dough according to the recipe directions. Divide the dough into quarters. Roll one part at a time on a lightly floured surface until paper-thin.

Roll the dough up like a jelly roll and slice ¼-inch-thick slices. Unroll the noodles and dry on a towel for 30 minutes or longer. Heat 6 quarts of salted water to boiling in a large kettle. Float 1 tablespoon of cooking oil on the surface of the water. Carefully add the noodles and boil gently for 5 minutes or until done to your taste. Drain well. Place the noodles in a heated bowl or platter. Add the butter and some freshly ground black pepper and toss with a fork and spoon until the butter melts. Sprinkle with the cheese and toss to coat. Serve immediately.

Serve this dish as a first course, pasta course or as an accompaniment to a main dish.

Makes 3 or 4 servings, depending upon how thinly the noodles have been rolled.

white clam sauce
salsa bianca alla vongole

18 fresh cherrystone clams
1 tablespoon butter
1 tablespoon olive oil
1 tablespoon flour
¾ cup water or clam juice
¼ teaspoon dried oregano,
  crumbled

¼ teaspoon dried sweet basil,
  crumbled
¼ teaspoon garlic powder
Salt and pepper to taste
1 tablespoon chopped parsley

Scrub the clams well under running water. Place on a baking sheet and bake at 450°F until the clams open. Remove the clams from the shells and chop. Reserve the juice for the sauce or for another use. Heat the butter and oil in a medium saucepan. Stir in the flour and cook, stirring constantly, for 2 minutes. Gradually stir the water or clam juice into the flour mixture.

Mix well and continue to cook until thickened. Add the clams and seasonings and simmer 2 minutes. Add the parsley and serve over hot cooked spaghetti.

Makes 3 to 4 servings.

ziti with sausage and cream sauce
ziti con sugo di salsiccia

2 tablespoons olive oil
3 tablespoons butter or
  margarine
¼ cup chopped onion
1 pound Italian sweet sausage
  (casing removed)

1 cup heavy cream
½ teaspoon salt
¼ teaspoon pepper
1 package (1 pound) ziti
¼ cup grated Parmesan
  cheese

Heat the butter and oil in a large skillet. Add the onion and sauté over moderate heat 2 minutes. Add the sausage and cook, crumbling with a fork, until lightly browned (about 10 minutes). Reduce the heat to low and add the cream, salt, and pepper and continue to cook, stirring until thickened. Do not boil.

Meanwhile, cook the ziti in boiling salted water until tender. Drain well. Transfer to a serving bowl and toss with the sauce and sprinkle with cheese. Serve hot.

Makes 4 servings.

spaghetti with sauce and italian-style meatballs

spaghetti con salsa di pomodori e polpette italani

meatballs

1 pound lean ground beef
½ cup Italian-style bread crumbs
1 egg, slightly beaten
1 tablespoon dried onion flakes
Salt and pepper
3 tablespoons cooking oil

tomato sauce

2 tablespoons olive oil
1 medium onion, chopped
1 clove garlic, minced
1 can (28 ounces) Italian-style peeled tomatoes
1 can (6 ounces) tomato paste
¾ cup water (or refill tomato-paste can)
1½ teaspoons mixed Italian herbs
1 teaspoon sugar
½ cup dry red wine

plus one of the following:

½ pound Italian sausage, cut in 1-inch pieces and browned

or

½ pound stewing beef, cut in 1½-inch cubes and browned in oil

or

1½ cups leftover cooked pork roast, cut in 1½-inch cubes

or

1 (4-ounce) can sliced mushrooms, drained

spaghetti

12 ounces thin spaghetti
4½ quarts boiling salted water
1 tablespoon cooking oil

First make the meatballs. Combine the ground beef, bread crumbs, eggs, onion flakes, and salt and pepper. Mix well and form into meatballs the size of a walnut. Brown in a medium-sized skillet in the cooking oil. Drain.

Next make the tomato sauce. Heat the olive oil in a large saucepan. Add the onion and garlic and sauté 5 minutes. Puree the tomatoes in a blender or force through a sieve. Add to the onion mixture with the tomato paste, water, seasonings and wine. Bring to a boil and reduce the heat to low. Add the meatballs and/or more of the items from the *plus section*. Simmer covered for 1 to 1½ hours or until thick.

Bring the salted water to a boil. Float the cooking oil on the surface of the water. Add the spaghetti and stir with a fork to prevent sticking. Cook according to the package directions and drain. To serve in the Italian manner, separate the meats from the sauce. Toss the sauce and the spaghetti together to coat lightly.

Serve the meats on a platter so that guests can serve themselves. Pass the grated Parmesan cheese.

Makes 4 servings.

baked lasagna

ravioli

little meat pies
ravioli

pasta
**1 double recipe Egg Noodles
(see Index)**

filling
**¾ pound meat-loaf mix
¼ cup dry bread crumbs**

**2 tablespoons grated
Parmesan cheese
1 egg
1 tablespoon dehydrated
parsley flakes
½ teaspoon garlic salt
¼ teaspoon pepper**

Prepare the pasta according to the recipe and let rest covered 15 minutes. Combine the filling ingredients in a bowl and mix well. Refrigerate until ready to use.

Divide the dough into 8 pieces. Roll one piece at a time on a lightly floured surface, keeping the remainder of the dough tightly covered. Roll the dough as thin as possible. If using a pasta machine to roll the dough, roll it to slightly less than a 1/16th of an inch thick. Cut the dough into 2-inch squares. Place 1 teaspoon of filling in the center of ½ of the squares. Top with the remainder of the squares. Press the edges together tightly to seal. Moisten the edges with a little water if necessary to ensure a tight seal. Dust a cookie sheet lightly with cornmeal. Place the ravioli on the sheet and refrigerate, covered, or freeze until ready to cook.

To cook, heat 4 quarts of water to boiling. Add 1 tablespoon of salt, and float 1 tablespoon of cooking oil on the surface of the water. Drop the ravioli into the water a few at a time and stir to prevent them from sticking to the bottom of the pan. Reduce the heat so that the water boils gently and cook for approximately 12 minutes or until tender. Drain. Serve hot with your favorite tomato or meat sauce and grated cheese or toss with melted butter and freshly grated Parmesan cheese.

Makes about 96 ravioli or 6 to 8 servings.

Note: Any leftover filling can be fried and added to the meat sauce for the ravioli. Any of the other fillings used in this section for manicotti or tortellini can be used instead of the meat filling given here.

stuffed
rigatoni
rigatoni ripieni

Cook a pound of rigatoni to be sure you have enough, since they break very easily. Eat any leftover unstuffed rigatoni with marinara sauce.

sauce

4 tablespoons olive oil
2 pounds meat-loaf mixture (ground beef, veal, and pork)
4 cloves garlic, peeled and chopped
½ cup finely chopped celery
½ cup finely chopped carrots
½ cup finely chopped green pepper
¼ cup finely chopped parsley
1 medium onion, finely chopped

1 6-ounce can tomato paste
¾ cup water
1 28-ounce can peeled Italian tomatoes
2 teaspoons sugar
1 teaspoon salt
½ teaspoon pepper
½ teaspoon dried sweet basil, crumbled
½ teaspoon dried oregano, crumbled

pasta and filling

1 pound rigatoni No. 28
2 10-ounce packages frozen chopped spinach, thawed
¼ cup grated Parmesan cheese

½ cup plain dry bread crumbs
2 eggs
Salt and pepper
1 clove garlic, peeled and minced

topping

½ cup grated Parmesan cheese

First make the sauce:

Heat 2 tablespoons of oil in a heavy skillet and add the meat and 3 cloves of garlic. Sauté slowly, without browning, until the meat loses its pink color. Drain and reserve ½ of the meat mixture for the pasta stuffing. In a Dutch oven, heat the rest of the oil and sauté the celery, carrot, green pepper, parsley and onion and 1 clove of garlic over medium heat until limp. Add the tomato paste and water. Sieve the tomatoes or puree in the blender and add to the sauce. Add ½ of the cooked meat and the seasonings. Bring to a boil. Reduce the heat to low and simmer 1½ to 2 hours.

Meanwhile, prepare the pasta and stuff it. In a large kettle, bring 4½ quarts of salted water to a boil over high heat. Float 1 tablespoon of cooking oil on the surface of the water. Add the rigatoni and stir well. Reduce the heat to medium-high and cook, stirring occasionally, for approximately 12 minutes or until almost done. Drain well and rinse with cold water. Squeeze the spinach in a sieve until dry. Combine the spinach, remaining meat, bread crumbs, eggs, salt, pepper and garlic and mix well. Stuff the rigatoni with the mixture, using a pastry tube or your fingers. Lightly grease a 13 × 9 × 2-inch baking dish. Layer the rigatoni and sauce in the baking dish. Sprinkle with the Parmesan cheese. Bake at 350°F for 30 to 45 minutes or until hot and bubbly.

Makes 8 servings.

Note: This casserole can be prepared in advance and refrigerated until baking time. Make it a day ahead, if you are serving it for a party.

31

cannelloni— venetian-style
cannelloni alla veneziana

pasta

½ recipe Egg Noodles
(see Index)

4 quarts boiling salted water
1 tablespoon oil

filling

1 large onion, chopped
1 clove garlic, minced
2 tablespoons olive oil
1 10-ounce package frozen
chopped spinach, thawed
2½ cups ground cooked ham

2 eggs, beaten
¾ teaspoon dried oregano,
crumbled
½ teaspoon salt
¼ teaspoon pepper

sauce

⅓ cup butter or margarine
⅓ cup all-purpose flour
½ teaspoon salt
Dash of nutmeg
Dash of white pepper
1 cup chicken broth

1 cup light cream
½ cup grated Parmesan or
Romano cheese
1 cup grated white cheddar or
Swiss cheese

Prepare the pasta according to the recipe. Allow to rest, covered, and roll on a lightly floured surface into sheets 1/16th of an inch thick and cut into 4 × 4-inch pieces. Allow to dry on lightly floured cookie sheets for 30 minutes. Float the oil on the surface of the water. Cook the pasta in the boiling water for 5 to 7 minutes or until al dente. Drain well and pat dry with paper towels.

Next make the filling. Sauté the onions and garlic in the oil until tender. Press the thawed spinach firmly in a strainer to remove all the water. Combine the onion mixture, spinach, ham, eggs and seasonings in a large bowl and mix well. Fill the noodles with 3 tablespoons of the filling and roll jelly-roll fashion to form a cylinder. Place in a single layer in a shallow baking dish.

Next make the sauce: In a medium-sized saucepan, melt the butter. Blend in the flour and seasonings. Cook, stirring constantly, until bubbly. Add the chicken broth and cream, all at one time, stirring well. Cook over moderate heat, stirring constantly, until thickened and smooth. Remove from the heat and add the cheese. Stir until the cheese has melted. Pour the sauce evenly over the cannelloni. Bake in a 350°F oven for 30 minutes. Garnish with finely chopped parsley and paprika.

Makes 15 stuffed noodles (serves 4 to 5).

spaghetti pancake
spaghettini frittatine

This recipe is a good way to use up leftover cooked spaghetti. Delicious served with fried Italian sausage, peppers and onions!

2 eggs
2 tablespoons finely minced
onion
½ teaspoon dried oregano,
crumbled
½ teaspoon salt

⅛ teaspoon pepper
3½ cups cold cooked spaghetti
3 tablespoons butter or
margarine
2 tablespoons grated
Parmesan cheese

In a medium mixing bowl, beat together the eggs, onion, oregano, salt and pepper. Add the spaghetti and toss well to coat. In a medium skillet, heat 2 tablespoons of the butter over moderate heat until the foam subsides. Add the spaghetti mixture and sprinkle with the cheese. Cook until the bottom is lightly browned. Turn out onto a plate. Heat the remaining tablespoon of butter in the pan. Slide the spaghetti pancake back into the pan, uncooked side down. Cook until lightly browned. Cut into 4 pieces and serve.

baked lasagna

lasagna alla forno

pasta

3 quarts water
2 teaspoons salt
1 tablespoon vegetable oil
8 ounces lasagna noodles

sauce

1 pound ground beef
2 mild Italian sausage links
   (with casing removed)
1 tablespoon olive oil
1 medium onion, finely diced
1 clove garlic, minced
1 28-ounce can peeled Italian
   tomatoes

1 6-ounce can tomato paste
½ teaspoon dried oregano,
   crumbled
½ teaspoon dried sweet basil,
   crumbled
1 teaspoon sugar

filling

8 ounces ricotta or pot cheese
8 ounces mozzarella cheese,
   thinly sliced

½ cup freshly grated
   Parmesan cheese

In a large kettle, combine the water and salt. Float the 1 tablespoon of oil on the surface of the water. Bring to a boil. Slowly add the lasagna noodles, a few at a time, and cook 15 minutes. Drain and rinse with cold water.

Meanwhile, brown the ground beef and sausages in a large skillet. Remove from the pan and pour the drippings away. Add the olive oil to the skillet and sauté the onion and garlic over low heat for 5 minutes. Add the tomatoes, broken up with a fork, the tomato paste and seasonings. Stir well and add the meat to the sauce. Cook over low heat for 40 minutes or until thick.

Lightly grease a 13 × 9 × 2-inch baking dish. Ladle approximately ¾ cup of the sauce into the pan. Top with ⅓ of the noodles. Dot with ½ of the riccota and ½ of the mozzarella. Add a layer of sauce and ⅓ of the noodles and the remaining ricotta and mozzarella. Top with more sauce and then the remaining noodles. Top with remaining sauce and sprinkle with the Parmesan cheese. Bake at 350°F for 30 minutes or until heated through. Serve with garlic bread and green salad.

Makes 6 servings.

pasta muffs
manicotti

This recipe only looks long! Really, stuffed manicotti are quite easy and offer a great deal of variety. These noodles can be prepared ahead and baked just before serving. In using this recipe, select the noodle or substitute of your choice and select *one* of the fillings. Top with the sauce and bake.

pasta

12 packaged manicotti shells
Boiling water
or 12 prepared entrée crêpes
or 12 cooked homemade manicotti noodles, 6 inches square (see index for Egg Noodles)

filling I

1 pound riccotta cheese or pot cheese
1 cup grated mozzarella cheese (¼ pound)
¼ cup grated Parmesan cheese
1 tablespoon dehydrated parsley flakes
1 egg, lightly beaten
½ teaspoon salt
¼ teaspoon white pepper
¼ teaspoon garlic powder

filling II

1 pound riccotta cheese or pot cheese
¼ cup grated Parmesan cheese
1 tablespoon dehydrated parsley flakes
3 links Italian sweet sausage, removed from the casing, cooked and chopped
1 egg, lightly beaten
¼ teaspoon salt
⅛ teaspoon pepper

filling III

1 medium onion, minced
1 clove garlic, peeled and chopped
2 tablespoons butter or margarine
1 10-ounce package frozen chopped spinach, thawed and pressed dry in a sieve
½ cup finely chopped chicken
1 teaspoon lemon juice
½ teaspoon salt
¼ teaspoon ground nutmeg
1 pound riccotta cheese
1 egg, lightly beaten

filling IV

2 tablespoons olive oil
1 small onion, chopped
½ pound ground beef
¼ pound Italian sweet sausage
¼ cup marinara sauce
¼ cup Italian style bread crumbs
1 cup grated mozzarella cheese (¼ pound)
½ tablespoon dehydrated chopped parsley flakes
Salt and pepper

sauce

3 cups marinara sauce
½ cup water (omit the water if using crêpes or homemade noodles)
3 tablespoons grated Parmesan cheese

If using the manicotti shells, cover with boiling water and let stand 5 minutes (of course you may cook the manicotti noodles in boiling salted water before stuffing, but it really isn't necessary and they break very easily when cooked and stuffed). Drain and rinse in cold water. Set aside while making the filling of your choice.

For fillings I and II combine all of the ingredients and mix well. For filling III, sauté the onion and garlic in the butter or margarine until transparent. Add the rest of the ingredients and mix well. For filling IV, heat the oil in a medium skillet. Add the onion, ground beef and sausage and cook over moderate heat until the meat is lightly browned. Stir frequently and break up the meat into small pieces. Drain well and remove from the heat. Allow to cool 5 minutes. Add the remaining ingredients and mix well.

Combine the marinara sauce and water (omit the water if using crepes or homemade noodles) in a medium saucepan and heat on low while stuffing the noodles. Stuff each shell or pancake with ⅓ to ½ cup of filling. Pour ¾ cup of the heated sauce into a 13 × 9 × 2-inch baking dish and tilt to coat lightly. Place the stuffed noodles in the dish. Top with remaining sauce. If using the manicotti noodles, cover with foil and bake 45 minutes at 375°F. Uncover and sprinkle with the Parmesan cheese and bake 5 more minutes. If using crepes or homemade noodles, bake at 350°F for 30 minutes, uncovered. Sprinkle with the grated Parmesan and bake 5 more minutes.

Serve with a green salad and garlic bread.

Makes 6 servings.

egg noodles—charcoal makers style

eggs, cheese and poultry

eggs in purgatory
uova in purgatorio

1 tablespoon olive oil
¼ cup onion, finely chopped
2 tablespoons chopped green
   pepper
1 tablespoon chopped parsley
Garlic salt and pepper, to
   taste
1 can (16 ounces) peeled
   Italian plum tomatoes,
   broken up
8 eggs
4 large slices toasted buttered
   Italian bread

Heat the oil in a medium skillet. Sauté the onion and green pepper until
limp. Add the parsley, and sauté 2 minutes. Add the garlic salt and
pepper and the tomatoes. Bring to a boil, then reduce the heat to simmer
and cook for 15 minutes. Bring the mixture to a boil once again. Break
the eggs into a saucer, one at a time, and slide into the sauce mixture.
Reduce the heat to low, cover the pan and poach to the desired degree of
doneness. Serve 2 eggs per serving on a slice of buttered, toasted Italian
bread.
Makes 4 servings.

eggs– florentine– style

uova alla florentine

1 pound fresh spinach
A pinch of salt

3 tablespoons butter or
  margarine

cheese sauce

3 tablespoons butter
3 tablespoons flour
Salt
White pepper

1 cup hot chicken broth
½ cup light cream
¾ cup freshly grated
  Parmesan cheese

eggs

6 eggs
Boiling salted water
A few drops white vinegar

Wash the spinach, remove coarse stems and discard undesirable leaves. Place the wet spinach in a saucepan with a tight-fitting lid. Set aside.

Next, prepare the cheese sauce. Melt the butter in a medium saucepan. Add the flour, salt and pepper and cook until bubbly. Add the chicken broth and cream and cook until thickened, stirring constantly. Remove from the heat and stir in the cheese. Keep the sauce warm.

Heat 1½ inches of salted water to boiling in a medium skillet. Add a few drops of vinegar and poach the eggs in the water to the desired degree of doneness. Meanwhile, sprinkle the spinach lightly with salt and steam over low heat 5 minutes. Drain. Place the spinach in a warm serving dish. Remove the eggs from the skillet with a slotted spoon and place on top of the spinach. Pour the sauce over the eggs and spinach. Serve immediately.

Makes 3 to 4 servings.

eggs and sausage

frittata con salsicce

4 links Italian sausage (casing
  removed)
2 tablespoons chopped green
  pepper
2 tablespoons chopped onion
3 tablespoons butter or
  margarine
4 eggs
Salt and pepper

Fry the sausage in a skillet, breaking up with a slotted spoon. When lightly browned, remove from the pan. In a 10-inch skillet, sauté the green pepper and onion in the butter until limp. Beat the eggs well, with salt and pepper to taste. Add the eggs and sausage to the skillet and cook over moderate heat, lifting the cooked egg occasionally with a spatula to let the uncooked egg flow to the bottom of the pan. When lightly browned and set, flip the omelet and cook until lightly browned.

Slide onto a platter and cut in wedges to serve.

Makes 4 servings.

zucchini omelet
frittata di zucchini

¼ cup olive oil or cooking oil
1 medium zucchini squash,
   thinly sliced
¼ cup onion, finely chopped
1 large tomato, peeled and
   finely chopped
¼ teaspoon dried oregano,
   crumbled
Salt and pepper
6 eggs
½ cup grated provolone or
   mozzarella cheese
   (optional)

Heat the oil in a 10-inch skillet over medium-high heat. Add the zucchini and onion and sauté until lightly browned. Add the tomato, oregano and salt and pepper and sauté to evaporate the liquid. Beat the eggs together well. Pour over the vegetable mixture and cook as you would an omelet, lifting the cooked egg and allowing the uncooked egg to flow to the bottom of the pan, until the top is almost set and the bottom is lightly browned. Sprinkle with the cheese (if used), cover and cook over low heat until the top of the omelet is set and the cheese is melted. Slide onto a platter, cut in wedges and serve.

Makes 4 servings.

eggs—florentine-style

zucchini omelet

spinach omelet

frittata alla florentine

1 10-ounce package frozen chopped spinach
3 tablespoons olive oil
¼ cup onion, finely chopped
1 clove garlic, minced
1 medium-sized tomato, peeled and chopped
½ teaspoon dried sweet basil, crumbled
4 eggs
½ teaspoon salt
⅛ teaspoon pepper
3 tablespoons olive oil

Cook the spinach following the package directions. Drain very well. In a medium saucepan, heat the 3 tablespoons of oil and sauté the onion and garlic until tender. Add the tomato, spinach and sweet basil and mix well.

Cook, stirring constantly, over medium heat for 3 minutes. Beat the eggs lightly until just mixed. Combine with the spinach mixture and salt and pepper and mix well. Heat the remaining 3 tablespoons of oil, in a 9-inch skillet with an ovenproof handle, until sizzling. Pour in the omelet mixture and cook covered for 10 minutes. The omelet should be fairly firm. Place the omelet under a hot broiler for 1 or 2 minutes to cook the top of the omelet.

Cut in wedges and serve.

Makes 4 servings.

fonduta

1 pound Fontina cheese (or Gruyère or Emmenthaler if Fontina is unavailable)
1 cup milk
4 eggs
Salt and white pepper, to taste
¼ cup white wine
1 canned white truffle, very thinly sliced (optional)
Bread sticks or 1 large loaf of crisp Italian bread, cut into chunks

Shred the cheese and place in a mixing bowl and stir in 1 cup of milk. Let stand 30 minutes. Beat together the eggs, salt, and white pepper. Beat the wine into the egg mixture. Blend the egg mixture into the cheese, mixing well. Cook in the top of a double boiler over gently boiling water, stirring constantly until the cheese melts and the mixture is smooth and slightly thickened.

Pour into a chafing dish or fondue pot (turn the burner down as far as it will go without going out or the cheese will burn) and serve, garnished with the truffle if desired. Serve the bread in a basket with fondue forks so that your guests can dip in the manner of Swiss fondue.

Makes 5 to 6 servings as a snack or hors d'oeuvre.

Note: Fonduta may also be served in warm ramekins, surrounded by crisp toast triangles. This dish may also be served as a main course for 4 people, accompanied by cubes of ham and assorted raw vegetables.

country pie

torta di rocotta e spinaci

2 tablespoons butter or margarine
½ cup chopped onion
1 10-ounce package frozen chopped spinach, thawed
1 pound ricotta cheese
½ cup grated Parmesan cheese
2 eggs, beaten
¾ teaspoon garlic salt
¼ teaspoon white pepper
¼ teaspoon ground nutmeg
1 9-inch unbaked pie shell

Heat the butter in a small skillet. Sauté the onion until tender. Drain the spinach well in a sieve and press with a spoon to remove all the liquid. In a mixing bowl, combine the spinach, sautéed onions, ricotta, Parmesan cheese, eggs and seasonings and mix well. Pour into the pie shell and bake at 375°F for 45 minutes. Serve hot.

Makes 4 to 6 servings.

fried cheese and rice balls

suppli al telefono

(literally it means telephone wires)

2½ cups water
2 teaspoons chicken broth granules
1 cup long-grain white rice
¼ cup grated Parmesan cheese
1 tablespoon dehydrated parsley flakes
1 egg, lightly beaten
15 ½-inch cubes mozzarella cheese
½ cup dry bread crumbs
Oil for frying

Combine the water and chicken broth granules in a saucepan. Bring to a boil, add the rice and stir well. Cover, reduce the heat to low and cook 25 to 30 minutes or until all the liquid is absorbed and the rice is very tender and a little sticky. Cool for 1 hour in the refrigerator. Combine the rice, Parmesan cheese, parsley flakes, and egg and mix well. Place a heaping tablespoon of the rice in the palm of your hand. Then place a cheese cube in the center of the rice. Add ½ of a tablespoon of rice mixture on top of the cheese cube and form into a ball, pressing well to make sure it holds together. Roll in dry bread crumbs. Continue until all of the rice has been used.

Heat 3 inches of oil in a medium saucepan to 365°F. Fry the rice balls 3 or 4 at a time until golden. Drain on absorbent paper and place in a warm oven until all the rice balls are fried. Serve with tomato or marinara sauce if desired.

Makes about 15 rice balls, or 4 servings.

baked chicken with marinara sauce

pollo alla forno con salsa marinara

1 2½- to 3-pound broiler-fryer chicken, cut-up
½ cup all-purpose flour
1 teaspoon salt
¼ teaspoon pepper
3 tablespoons butter or margarine
1 15½-ounce can marinara sauce *or* 2 cups homemade marinara sauce
1 teaspoon dried dillweed
2 tablespoons grated Parmesan cheese

Combine the flour, salt and pepper in a brown paper bag. Add the chicken a few pieces at a time and shake until coated with the flour mixture. Place the chicken in a single layer in a shallow baking dish. Dot with the butter. Bake at 450°F for 25 minutes. Remove from the oven. Pour the sauce over the chicken. Sprinkle with the dillweed and cheese. Reduce the heat to 350°F and bake 25 minutes more.

Serve hot or cold. This makes a great picnic dish.

Makes 4 servings.

chicken with garlic and oil

pollo con aglio e olio

1 2½- to 3-pound frying
  chicken, cut-up
½ cup olive oil
4 medium potatoes
6 medium carrots
1 medium onion
2 cloves garlic, peeled and
  chopped
Juice of 1 lemon
Salt and freshly ground black
  pepper

Wash the chicken well and pat dry. Pour the olive oil into the bottom of a 14 × 10 × 2½-inch pan or other large roasting pan. Dip the chicken pieces into the oil and turn to coat. Turn the chicken skin-side-up and distribute evenly in the pan. Peel the potatoes, quarter and cut into ½-inch-thick wedges. Arrange around the chicken. Peel the carrots, cut in half lengthwise and then into sticks. Add to the pan. Peel the onion and sliver. Distribute among the vegetables in the pan. Sprinkle the garlic and lemon juice over all. Salt lightly and grind fresh pepper over the whole pan. Bake at 350°F for 1 hour, basting every 15 minutes, or until the chicken is cooked through and the vegetables are tender.

Makes 4 servings.

chicken-lake como–style

pollo alla lac como

1 3-pound broiler-fryer
  chicken
1 tablespoon olive oil
1 clove garlic
½ teaspoon salt
½ teaspoon leaf sage,
  crumbled

3 thin slices salt pork
Juice of 1 fresh lemon
¼ teaspoon freshly ground
  pepper

Wash the chicken well in cold water and pat dry. With kitchen string, tie the legs together. Place another piece of string around the chicken and tie the wings so that they stay close to the sides of the bird. Rub the outside of the chicken with olive oil. Place the chicken in a shallow baking dish, breast-side-up. Peel the clove of garlic and sprinkle with the salt. Crush with the side of a heavy kitchen knife. Rub the chicken with the garlic and the crumbled sage. Lay the slices of salt pork over the chicken. Preheat the oven to 350°F. Roast for 1 hour. Remove from the oven and pour the lemon juice mixed with the pepper over the chicken. Return to the oven and roast for 30 minutes more, basting occasionally. The chicken is done when the skin is well browned and the leg joint moves easily when pulled. Remove to a platter, cut and remove the strings and carve. Serve with the pan juices.

Makes 4 servings.

Variations: Pan-roasted potatoes are an excellent accompaniment to this dish!! Peel four small potatoes and rub with olive oil. Place around the chicken at the beginning of the roasting time. If you prefer vegetables, try artichoke hearts with this dish. Defrost a 9-ounce package of artichoke hearts and place around the chicken when the lemon juice and pepper are added to the chicken. Baste when you baste the chicken.

chicken in the style of florence

pollo alla fiorentina

1 2½- to 3-pound chicken
2 tablespoons olive oil
1 medium onion, chopped
1 clove garlic, minced
4 large fresh tomatoes, peeled and chopped (canned tomatoes may be substituted if drained and chopped)
4 large, chopped green olives
½ teaspoon dried sweet basil, crumbled
½ teaspoon dried oregano, crumbled
½ teaspoon celery salt
¼ teaspoon pepper
4 bay leaves

Wash the chicken, drain and pat dry. Cut the chicken into quarters. Cut 4 (10-inch) pieces of aluminum foil and grease with olive oil. Place a piece of chicken in the center of each piece of foil. Combine the onion, garlic, tomatoes, green olives, sweet basil, oregano, celery salt, and pepper. Mix well. Spoon some of the sauce over each piece of chicken. Add 1 bay leaf to each package. Place on a cookie sheet and bake at 425°F for 40 minutes. Serve from the packages with a green salad and garlic bread.

Makes 4 servings.

fried chicken, italian-style

fritto di pollo

2½ pounds chicken parts (drumsticks, thighs, breasts and wings)
⅓ cup flour
½ teaspoon seasoned salt
¼ teaspoon pepper
2 eggs
2 tablespoons milk
⅔ cup dry bread crumbs
⅓ cup grated Parmesan cheese
Oil for frying
Parsley
Lemon slices

Wash the chicken and pat dry. Combine the flour and seasoned salt and pepper in a paper bag and shake the chicken a few pieces at a time in the flour mixture until lightly coated. Beat the eggs and milk together in a shallow bowl. On a piece of waxed paper combine the bread crumbs and Parmesan cheese. Dip the floured chicken pieces in the egg and then the bread crumb mixture, coating well. Heat 1½ inches of oil in a heavy skillet over moderate heat. Fry the chicken a few pieces at a time until golden brown. Drain on paper towels. Place on a baking sheet and bake at 350°F for 15 to 20 minutes or until the juices run clear when pierced with a knife.

Garnish with parsley and lemon slices and serve with basil flavored tomato sauce if you wish.

Makes 4 servings.

Picture on opposite page: fried chicken italian-style

chicken breasts, piedmont-style

petti di pollo alla piedmontese

4 chicken breast halves
  (about 1½ pounds total)
2 tablespoons flour
¾ teaspoon salt
¼ teaspoon pepper
2 tablespoons butter or margarine
½ cup sliced fresh mushrooms
1 tablespoon butter or
  margarine
4 thin slices Fontina or Swiss
  cheese

Skin and bone the chicken breasts. Place between sheets of waxed paper and flatten with a heavy skillet on a hard surface. Combine the flour, salt and pepper and coat the chicken with the mixture. Heat the butter in a heavy skillet. Sauté the chicken in the butter 5 to 6 minutes on each side or until golden and cooked through.

Meanwhile, in a small skillet, sauté the mushrooms in the 1 tablespoon of butter until tender. Place the chicken in a single layer in a small ovenproof casserole. Top with the mushrooms and then the cheese. Broil just until the cheese is melted.

Makes 4 servings.

chicken livers and vegetables

fegatini di pollo con vegetale

2 tablespoons butter or
  margarine
1 medium onion, peeled and
  sliced
1 clove garlic, minced
1 medium green pepper,
  cleaned and cut into chunks
¼ pound mushrooms, sliced
½ cup prosciutto, cut into
  strips
1 pound chicken livers
¼ cup flour
Salt and pepper
¼ cup butter or margarine
2 tablespoons dry sherry
½ cup chicken broth
2 tablespoons finely chopped
  parsley

In a small skillet, heat the butter over moderate heat until the foam subsides. Add the onion, garlic, green pepper, mushrooms and prosciutto and sauté over low heat while preparing the chicken livers.

Drain the chicken livers well in a colander. Combine the flour, salt and pepper on waxed paper. Dip the chicken livers in the flour mixture to coat well. Heat the ¼ cup of butter in a large skillet. Add the chicken livers and cook over moderate heat until browned. Drain the fat from the pan. Add the sherry and chicken broth. Cover and cook over low heat for 5 minutes. Place the chicken livers in a serving dish. Top with the vegetables and sprinkle with parsley. Serve with rice.

Makes 4 servings.

turkey tetrazzini
tacchino tetrazzini

4 tablespoons butter or margarine
3 tablespoons olive oil
½ pound fresh mushrooms, cleaned and sliced
4 tablespoons flour
2 cups chicken broth
1 cup heavy cream
2 tablespoons dry sherry
¾ cup grated Parmesan cheese
⅛ teaspoon ground nutmeg
3 cups cubed cooked turkey
½ pound spaghetti or vermicelli, cooked and drained
2 tablespoons butter
¼ cup Italian-style bread crumbs

In a large saucepan, heat the butter and oil. Add the mushrooms and sauté for 5 minutes. Remove the mushrooms with a slotted spoon and reserve. Add the flour to the pan juices and stir to form a roux. Cook until bubbly. Slowly add the chicken broth and cook until thickened. Remove from the heat and add the cream, sherry, Parmesan, and nutmeg and stir until the cheese melts. Add the turkey and reserved mushrooms and stir well. Combine with the cooked spaghetti and turn into a greased 13 × 9 × 2-inch baking dish (or use the 3-quart baking dish of your choice). Melt the 2 tablespoons of butter and toss with the bread crumbs. Sprinkle over the casserole. Bake at 375°F for 25 to 30 minutes.

Makes 6 servings.

chicken in the style of florence

fish

shrimp with marinara sauce

fish soup
zuppa di pesce

Although this dish is called a soup, it is really more of a stew. Serve with lots of crisp-crusted Italian bread or bread sticks.

3 quarts water
1 tablespoon salt
1 large onion, sliced
1 bay leaf
3 stalks celery (with tops),
    chopped
1 1¼-pound lobster
½ pound shrimp
3 pounds fish heads, bones
    and trimmings
1 dozen clams
½ cup olive oil
2 cloves garlic, peeled and
    minced
2 pounds fish fillets (any firm
    white fish can be used;
    select one or more kinds
    from this list of possibilities:
    red snapper, bass,
    rockfish, cod, haddock,
    flounder, or perch), cut into
    chunks
2 cups drained Italian-style
    tomatoes, broken up
1 cup dry white wine
¼ cup chopped parsley
¼ teaspoon thyme
1 teaspoon dried sweet basil,
    crumbled
Freshly ground pepper
A scant ¼ teaspoon of saffron

In a large stock pot (5 to 6 quarts), combine the water, salt, onion, bay leaf, and celery and bring to a boil. Add the lobster and return to a boil. Reduce the heat to low and cook 10 minutes. Add the shrimp and cook 5 minutes more. Remove the shrimp and lobster. Add the fish heads and trimmings and cook, uncovered, 1 hour. When the shrimp and lobster are cool enough to handle, remove the shrimp from the shells and add the shells to the stock. Remove the sand veins and discard.

Clean the lobster and remove the shell. Add the shell to the stock and cut the meat into large chunks. Scrub the clams and wash well to remove the grit. Add to the stock and cook 15 minutes. Remove from the pot and reserve.

In a Dutch oven, heat the olive oil. Add the garlic and sauté until lightly browned. Add the fish and brown in the oil. Add the tomatoes, wine, parsley, thyme, basil, and pepper and stir well.

Strain the fish stock through a fine sieve. You should have 2 quarts. Dissolve the saffron in the broth. Add to the fish and tomato mixture. Bring to a boil. Reduce the heat to low and cook 15 minutes. Add the lobster, shrimp and clams and cook 10 minutes more. Serve in large soup bowls.

shrimp with marinara sauce

scampi marinara

1 pound large shrimp (18 to 22)
1 quart water
Salt
1 bay leaf
1 slice lemon

sauce
2 tablespoons olive oil
½ cup chopped onion
1 clove garlic, minced
1½ cups Italian-style peeled plum tomatoes

¼ cup tomato puree
½ teaspoon sugar
½ teaspoon dried sweet basil, crumbled
Salt and pepper

garnish
2 tablespoons dry bread crumbs
2 tablespoons grated Parmesan cheese
1 tablespoon parsley, finely chopped

Peel and devein the shrimp. Combine the water, salt to taste, bay leaf and lemon in a large saucepan. Bring to a boil. Add the shrimp and bring the water rapidly to a boil and cook 5 minutes. Drain.

Heat the oil in a heavy skillet. Add the onion and garlic and sauté until tender. Break up the tomatoes, and add to the onion and garlic along with the tomato puree and seasonings. Reduce the heat to low and cook uncovered 20 minutes. Place the shrimp in a lightly greased au gratin dish. Top with the sauce. Combine the bread crumbs, cheese and parsley and sprinkle over the top of the shrimp and sauce. Preheat the oven to 450°F and bake for 10 minutes.

Makes 3 servings.

shrimp, lobster, and crab diavolo

gamberi, aragosta, e granchio fra diavolo

1 1¼-pound live lobster
1 pound king crab legs
2 pounds medium shrimp, raw
½ cup butter
2 tablespoons olive oil
2 cloves garlic, peeled and minced
⅛ teaspoon crushed red pepper
Juice of 1 lemon
2 tablespoons chopped parsley

Steam the lobster and crab legs and cool. Peel the shrimp, leaving the tails intact. Butterfly and remove the sand vein. Drain well. Remove the lobster and crab from the shell and slice. In a large heavy skillet, heat the butter and oil over moderate heat. Add the garlic and sauté for 2 minutes. Add the shrimp and pepper and sauté until the shrimp turns pink. Add the crab and lobster and heat through.

Sprinkle with the lemon juice and parsley and serve with garlic bread. Makes 4 to 5 servings.

Note: You may substitute any combination of shellfish that you prefer in this dish. Count on a 50 percent loss for shells (meaning: use 2 pounds raw shellfish, shells removed).

mixed fish fry
fritto misto di pesce

batter

3 large eggs
¼ cup olive oil
¼ cup all-purpose flour
¼ teaspoon dried rosemary,
   crumbled
¼ teaspoon dried sweet basil,
   crumbled
Salt and pepper

for the fish fry

1½ pounds fish fillets, shrimp,
   cleaned squid, clams,
   mussels or eel (if the fish is
   frozen, defrost and drain
   well)
½ cup flour
Salt and pepper
Oil for frying (half olive oil if
   possible)
Parsley, lemon wedges and
   quartered tomatoes

Beat the eggs until well-mixed with a wire whip. Add the olive oil and beat to mix well. Add the flour and seasonings and beat until a smooth batter is formed. Let stand 30 minutes and beat again before dipping the fish.

Rinse the fish and pat dry. Heat 3 inches of oil in a deep-fat fryer or 1 inch of oil in an electric skillet to 360°F. Dredge the fish in the flour, seasoned with salt and pepper. Coat well and shake off the excess. Dip the fish in the batter a few pieces at a time, and deep-fat fry until golden. Drain on absorbent paper. Keep warm until all the fish is cooked. Garnish with parsley and lemon wedges. Vegetables are also delicious cooked in this manner. Trim and slice 1 medium zucchini and ¼ pound of mushrooms and cut the amount of fish to be cooked to ¾ of a pound. Cook as above.

Makes 6 servings (if you are using only fish) or 4 servings (if you are frying fish and vegetables).

Serve with your favorite sauce or:

green sauce
salsa verde

½ cup mayonnaise
2 tablespoons chopped onion
1 teaspoon chopped capers
2 tablespoons lemon juice
2 teaspoons chopped chives
2 tablespoons chopped parsley

Combine all of the ingredients and mix well. Refrigerate 1 hour before serving.

fried squid
seppie fritto

3 pounds frozen squid
2 cups Italian-style bread
  crumbs
3 eggs, well-beaten
1 teaspoon salt
½ teaspoon pepper

Thaw the squid. Remove the tentacles by cutting them from the head and reserve. Remove and discard the head, chitinous pen and viscera. Wash thoroughly and drain. Cut the mantle into rings. Combine the bread crumbs, salt and pepper. Dip the tentacles and mantle rings first in the egg and then in the crumbs, coating well. Deep-fat fry at 350°F until golden brown.

Serve immediately with lemon wedges. Makes 4 to 5 servings.

rolled haddock fillets
involtini di pesce

1¼ pounds flounder or
  haddock fillets (4 to 5
  fillets)
1½ tablespoons butter
2 tablespoons chopped onion
2 tablespoons chopped celery
1 cup dry bread crumbs
1 tablespoon chopped parsley
2 tablespoons grated
  Parmesan cheese

½ teaspoon dried tarragon,
  crumbled
Salt and pepper
1 egg, beaten
2 tablespoons milk
½ of a lemon, thinly sliced
3 tablespoons butter

Wash the fish fillets, and pat dry. Heat the 1½ tablespoons of butter in a small skillet. Sauté the onion and celery in the butter until tender.

Remove from the heat. In a bowl, combine the bread crumbs, parsley, Parmesan cheese, tarragon and salt and pepper and mix well. Add the celery, onion and butter and mix. Beat the egg and milk and add to the crumb mixture and thoroughly combine. Pat about ⅓ cup of the crumb mixture on top of each fillet and roll up like a jelly roll. Fasten with toothpicks. Melt 1½ tablespoons of butter in an 8-inch baking dish. Place the fish rolls on end in the baking dish. Dot with the remaining butter and top with the lemon slices. Bake at 350°F for 30 minutes or until the fish is tender and flakes easily with a fork.

Makes 4 servings.

fillet of fish baked in tomato sauce
filetti di pesce con salsa di pomodori

Olive oil
1 pound haddock, cod or
  other white fish fillets, fresh
  or thawed and separated
1 8-ounce can tomato sauce
¼ teaspoon dried sweet basil,
  crumbled
Salt and pepper

Lightly grease a baking dish with olive oil. Arrange the fish fillets in the baking dish. Combine the tomato sauce, sweet basil, and salt and pepper and pour evenly over the fillets. Cover the dish with foil. Bake at 350°F for 15 minutes. Remove the foil and bake 15 more minutes or until the fish is tender and flakes with a fork.

Makes 4 servings.

meats

pork roast in chianti
arrosto di maiale con chianti

1 4-pound boned, rolled and
  tied pork roast
1½ cups Chianti wine
1 clove garlic, minced
2 tablespoons lemon juice
1 teaspoon dried rosemary,
  crumbled
1 teaspoon dried basil,
  crumbled
3 tablespoons olive oil
1 8-ounce can tomato sauce
Salt and pepper, to taste

Wipe the pork roast with a damp cloth. Place in a glass or porcelain container or a heavy-duty freezer bag. Combine the Chianti, garlic, lemon juice, rosemary, and basil and pour over the meat. Cover and marinate in the refrigerator for 24 hours, turning occasionally (if using a plastic bag, close with a twist-tie). Bring the roast to room temperature before cooking. Remove the roast from the marinade and pat dry. Reserve the marinade. Heat the oil in a large heavy Dutch oven. Brown the roast well on all sides. Combine the marinade and the tomato sauce, salt and pepper and pour over the meat. Bring to a boil and then reduce the heat to simmer. Cover and cook for 3 hours (the meat should be fork-tender). Place the roast on a platter and slice. Serve with the pan juices.
Makes 6 to 8 servings.

breaded pork chops
costatelle di maiale impanati

4 loin pork chops, 1-inch thick
Salt and pepper
1 large egg
2 tablespoons water
Bread crumbs
¼ cup clarified butter
½ teaspoon dried sage

Carefully trim the excess fat from the pork chops. Season with salt and pepper. Beat the egg and water. Dip the chops in the egg and then coat with the bread crumbs, pressing the crumbs firmly onto the chops. In a heavy skillet, heat the clarified butter over moderate heat. Crumble the sage and add to the butter. Add the chops and cook slowly until well-browned and done through.

Makes 4 servings.

Note: 1 pound of well-pounded veal cutlets can be substituted for the pork chops.

pork chops cacciatore
costatelle di maiale alla cacciatora

Polenta, gnocchi, rice or mashed potatoes goes well with this dish. It's delicious with the gravy!!

2 tablespoons olive oil
4 loin pork chops (1 pound)
1 small onion, sliced
1 clove garlic, minced
½ cup sliced green pepper
1 4-ounce can sliced
  mushrooms, drained
1 16-ounce can peeled
  tomatoes, broken up with a
  fork

2 tablespoons sherry
½ teaspoon dried oregano,
  crumbled
½ teaspoon dried basil,
  crumbled
½ teaspoon sugar
Salt and pepper

Heat the oil in a large skillet. Brown the chops well and remove from the skillet. Add the onion, garlic, and green pepper and sauté lightly over medium heat. Add the mushrooms, tomatoes, sherry, and seasonings. Bring the mixture to a boil. Return the chops to the skillet. Cover and simmer for 1 hour, or until the chops are tender. Serve with the pan juices.

Makes 4 servings.

sausage and vegetable bake
salsiccia con vegetali

1 pound Italian sweet sausage
  links
4 medium baking potatoes,
  peeled, quartered and cut
  in ½-inch wedges

1 large green pepper, cleaned
  and cut in thin strips
1 medium onion, peeled and
  slivered
Salt and pepper

Pour ½ inch of water into a 13 × 9 × 2-inch baking dish. Prick the sausage links in several places and cut apart. Evenly distribute the sausage links in the baking pan. Surround them with the potatoes, peppers and onions. Salt and pepper lightly. Bake at 350°F for 1 hour, basting occasionally, or until the sausages are browned and the potatoes are cooked through.

Makes 4 servings.

stuffed peppers
pepperonata imbottiti

4 medium bell peppers
1 pound ground beef
½ cup chopped onion
½ teaspoon garlic powder
1 teaspoon mixed Italian herbs, crumbled
Salt and pepper
1 16-ounce can stewed tomatoes
1 8-ounce can tomato sauce
¼ cup water
1 cup instant rice (or quick-cooking)
2 ounces thinly sliced mozzarella cheese

Cut the tops off of the peppers and remove the seeds and membranes. Parboil the peppers for 5 minutes and drain. Sauté the ground beef and onions until lightly browned in a large skillet, adding a little oil if the meat is very lean. Add the garlic powder, Italian herbs, salt and pepper, tomatoes, ½ of the can of tomato sauce, water and rice. Stir well. Bring to a boil, reduce the heat to low and cook, covered, 15 minutes. Place the peppers in a 2-quart casserole. Stuff with the meat mixture and spoon the remaining meat mixture around the peppers. Top with the remaining tomato sauce. Cover and cook 30 minutes, at 350°F. Uncover, top with the cheese and cook 10 more minutes.

Makes 4 servings.

beef rolls with tomato gravy
braciola con salsa

1¼ pounds very thinly sliced top round of beef (¼ inch thick)
¼ cup olive oil
1 medium onion, finely chopped
¾ cup Italian-style bread crumbs
3 tablespoons olive oil
2 tablespoons chopped onion
1½ cups canned Italian-style peeled plum tomatoes, broken up
½ cup tomato sauce
½ tablespoon dehydrated parsley flakes
½ teaspoon sugar
½ teaspoon oregano
Salt and pepper

Pound the meat well and cut into rectangular pieces approximately 4 × 6 inches. You should have 8 pieces, so vary the measurements accordingly. In a small skillet, heat the olive oil and sauté the onion until it is tender. Remove from the heat and add the bread crumbs and stir well. Place 2 tablespoons of the bread crumb mixture on each piece of steak and roll jelly-roll fashion to enclose the stuffing. Fasten with toothpicks. Heat the olive oil in a heavy skillet and brown the steak rolls. Place in a shallow baking dish. Add the onion and brown lightly. Add the remaining ingredients and stir well. Simmer for 15 to 20 minutes or until thickened. Pour over the steak rolls, cover and bake at 350°F for 1 hour.

Serve with mashed potatoes.

Makes 4 servings.

pizza burgers

beef stew
manzo stufato

2 tablespoons olive oil
2 slices bacon, chopped
½ cup chopped onion
½ cup sliced celery
1 clove garlic, minced
1¼ pounds lean stew beef, cut in 1-inch cubes
2 tablespoons chopped parsley
1 16-ounce can peeled tomatoes, broken up
½ cup water
1 teaspoon beef-broth granules

½ teaspoon dried sweet basil, crumbled
Salt and pepper
½ teaspoon sugar
3 medium carrots, peeled and sliced
3 medium potatoes, peeled and diced
¼ cup red wine
1½ cups sliced zucchini squash (unpeeled)

Heat the oil in a Dutch oven. Add the bacon and sauté until crisp. Remove the bacon from the pan with a slotted spoon and reserve. Add the onion, celery, and garlic and sauté 5 minutes. Remove with a slotted spoon and reserve. Add the stew beef and cook over moderate heat until well browned on all sides, stirring occasionally. Add the reserved ingredients, parsley, tomatoes, water, beef-broth granules and seasonings and cook covered over low heat for 1 hour. Add the carrots and potatoes and stir well. Cover and cook for 45 minutes. Add the wine and zucchini and stir well. Cook 15 more minutes or until the vegetables are tender.

Makes 4 servings.

milanese veal rolls

mixed boiled meats with green sauce

bollitti misti con salsa verde

meat pot

1 pound beef pot roast or
   brisket
1 pound veal shoulder
2 whole chicken legs
2 marrow bones, cracked
Water
2 bay leaves
1 onion
2 cloves
1 clove garlic
1 teaspoon salt
½ teaspoon sugar
4 peppercorns
½ teaspoon thyme
4 carrots, peeled and cut in
   half lengthwise
2 leeks, cleaned and cut in
   half lengthwise
½ pound cooked beef tongue
Parsley for garnish

green sauce

Juice of 1 fresh lemon
3 egg yolks
¼ teaspoon salt
½ cup olive oil
1 slice white bread, soaked in
   water and squeezed dry
½ teaspoon prepared mustard
1 clove garlic, peeled and
   mashed
½ cup chopped parsley
½ teaspoon dried sweet basil,
   crumbled
½ teaspoon dried oregano,
   crumbled

Place the beef, veal, chicken, and marrow bones in a large Dutch oven or stew pot. Cover with water. Add the bay leaves. Peel the onion and stud with cloves and add to the kettle. Peel the clove of garlic, sprinkle with the salt and mash with the blade of a knife. Add to the pot with the sugar, peppercorns, and thyme. Bring to a boil. Skim the foam from the surface of the liquid. Reduce the heat to low, cover and cook for 40 minutes. Remove the chicken, add the carrots and leeks, and cook for 30 more minutes.

Meanwhile, make the green sauce. Combine the lemon juice, egg yolks and salt in the jar of an electric blender. Blend on medium speed for 2 minutes. Add the oil a tablespoon at a time, blending well after each addition. Add the bread, mustard and garlic and blend 2 minutes. Pour into a serving bowl and stir in the parsley, sweet basil and oregano. Refrigerate until serving time.

Skin the chicken. Return to the pot along with the tongue and heat through. Remove the meats from the pot and slice. Arrange on a warm platter, garnish with parsley and serve with the green sauce. Reserve the broth for soups.

Serves 4 generously.

italian sausages and beans

salsiccie e fagioli

1 pound sweet or hot Italian
   sausage links
Cold water
2 tablespoons olive oil
¼ cup chopped onions

1 8-ounce can tomato sauce
2 16-ounce cans cannelli beans
   or kidney beans, drained
2 tablespoons chopped parsley

Prick the sausages well on all sides. Place in a large skillet and just barely cover with cold water. Cook over moderate heat, uncovered, until the water evaporates. Then cook, turning occasionally, until the sausages are browned on all sides. Remove from the pan and keep warm. Add the oil and onion to the skillet and sauté until tender. Add the tomato sauce and simmer 5 minutes. Add the beans and sausages to the pan and simmer for 15 minutes, stirring occasionally to prevent sticking.

Sprinkle with parsley and serve.

Makes 4 servings.

beef—parma-style
manzo parmigana

This is one of my mother's all-time favorite recipes (and mine too)!!

1½ pounds beef round steak
½ cup dry bread crumbs
⅓ cup grated Parmesan
   cheese
1 egg
2 tablespoons water
¼ cup flour
⅓ cup cooking oil
1 medium onion, minced

1 6-ounce can tomato paste
2 cups hot water
½ teaspoon dried marjoram,
   crumbled
1 teaspoon salt
¼ teaspoon pepper
½ pound mozzarella cheese,
   thinly sliced

Place the meat between sheets of waxed paper and pound with a heavy skillet on a hard surface until quite thin. Cut into serving-size pieces. Combine the bread crumbs and Parmesan cheese. Beat the egg and 2 tablespoons of water together. Dip the meat in the flour, turn to coat and shake off the excess. Dip the meat in the egg mixture and then in the crumb mixture. Pat the crumbs into the meat to coat well. Heat the oil in a heavy skillet over moderate heat.

Brown the meat on both sides. Remove from the pan. Add the onions and brown lightly. Add the tomato paste, hot water and seasonings. Stir well. Boil for 5 minutes. Place the meat in a shallow baking dish. Cover with the sauce; reserve ¾ cup. Top the meat with the mozzarella cheese and pour the remaining sauce over the cheese. Cover with aluminum foil and bake at 350°F for 2 hours.

Serve with pasta and a green salad.

Makes 4 to 5 servings.

meat loaf—italian-style
polpettone

1½ pounds meat-loaf mix
   (ground beef, pork and
   veal) *or* 1½ pounds lean
   ground beef
1 egg, lightly beaten
½ cup Italian-style bread
   crumbs
¼ cup chopped onion
½ teaspoon dried sweet basil,
   crumbled
½ teaspoon dried oregano,
   crumbled
Salt and pepper to taste
1 10½-ounce can pizza sauce
   with cheese
2 ounces thinly sliced
   mozzarella cheese

In a large bowl, combine the meat, egg, bread crumbs, onion, seasonings and one half of the can of pizza sauce. Mix well. Form into a large round loaf, and place in a 3-quart round casserole. Pour the remaining pizza sauce over the meat loaf. Bake at 350°F for 1¼ hours. Top with the sliced cheese and bake 5 more minutes. Remove from the oven and let stand 5 minutes before slicing.

Makes 6 servings (or 4 with a lot of good sandwiches for lunch).

pizza burgers

Although not authentically Italian, these burgers are quick and popular with the younger set!

1½ pounds ground beef
½ cup chopped onion

¾ teaspoon garlic salt
¼ teaspoon pepper

sauce
2 cups peeled Italian-style tomatoes, broken up with a fork
1 8-ounce can tomato sauce
¼ cup chopped canned mushrooms

1 teaspoon dried oregano, crumbled
6 large French rolls, split (or small individual French bread loaves)
8 ounces mozzarella cheese, sliced

Combine the ground beef, onion, garlic salt and pepper and form into 6 patties the size and shape of the rolls. Combine the tomatoes, tomato sauce, mushrooms, and oregano in a saucepan and heat. Broil the hamburgers until done to your liking. Place the hamburgers on the bottom half of the rolls. Top with some of the sauce, the sliced cheese and then garnish with an additional tablespoon of the sauce. Return to the broiler until the cheese melts.

Serve open face or topped with the other half of the roll.

Makes 6 servings.

stuffed zucchini
zucchini ripieni

4 medium zucchini squash (about ¾ pound each)
1 pound ground beef (or ½ pound beef and ½ pound sausage)
¼ cup olive oil
1 clove garlic, chopped
1 medium onion, chopped
½ cup green pepper, chopped
1 tablespoon chopped parsley

½ teaspoon dried oregano, crumbled
Salt and pepper
1 cup fresh bread crumbs from French or Italian bread
1¾ cups tomato sauce (divided)
¼ cup grated Parmesan cheese

Slice the zucchini in half lengthwise. Scoop out the pulp and chop. Sauté the ground beef (and sausage if used) in the olive oil until it loses its pink color. Add the garlic and onion and green pepper and cook 5 more minutes. Remove from the heat and add the squash pulp, parsley, oregano, salt and pepper, bread crumbs and ¼ cup of the tomato sauce. Mix well and stuff the squash shells with the mixture. Place in a shallow baking dish. Top with the remaining 1½ cups of tomato sauce and sprinkle with the cheese. Bake at 350°F for 40 minutes.

Makes 4 servings.

roast leg of lamb with rosemary
abbacchio al forno con rosmarino

1 5-pound whole leg of lamb
  or sirloin half leg of lamb
1 large clove of garlic
1 teaspoon dried rosemary,
  crumbled
1 teaspoon grated lemon peel
Salt and freshly ground black
  pepper
Olive oil

Wipe the meat with a damp cloth. Peel the garlic and rub over the surface of the lamb. Cut the garlic clove into slivers. Make 4 or 5 deep slashes in the meat and insert the garlic slivers. Rub the meat with the rosemary, lemon peel, and salt and pepper. Place in an open roasting pan on a trivet, fat-side-up.

Sprinkle with olive oil. Roast at 325°F for 3 hours or to an internal temperature of 180°F. Let stand for 10 minutes before carving. Peeled potatoes and carrots can be placed in the pan drippings for the last 1½ hours of cooking time, turning occasionally.

Makes 6 servings.

lamb chops— venetian-style
costatello d'agnello alla vincenza

2 tablespoons butter or
  margarine
2 tablespoons olive oil
4 lamb shoulder chops
  (approximately 2 pounds)
Salt and pepper to taste
1 medium onion
1¾ pound eggplant
3 tablespoons tomato paste
½ teaspoon dried sweet basil,
  crumbled
½ cup boiling water
½ 10-ounce package frozen
  peas
1 8½-ounce can artichoke
  bottoms (or substitute 1 can
  artichoke hearts), drained

Heat the butter and olive oil in a heavy skillet. Wipe the lamb chops with a damp cloth and season with salt and pepper. Sauté in the butter and oil approximately 4 minutes on a side, until well-browned and almost done. Remove from the pan and keep warm.

While the chops cook, peel the onion, quarter and separate the layers. Cut the stem from the eggplant, cut in half lengthwise and thinly slice. Add the onions to the skillet and sauté for 5 minutes. Add the eggplant. Combine the tomato paste, basil and boiling water. Stir well and add to the skillet. Bring to a boil, reduce the heat to low, cover and cook 15 minutes. Add the peas, artichoke bottoms (quartered) or artichoke hearts, and the lamb chops. Cook covered for 15 more minutes or until the vegetables are done through.

Makes 4 servings.

milanese veal rolls

rollini di vitella alla milanese

1½ pounds rump roast of veal
  or veal cutlet
Salt and pepper
Ground sage
4 slices prosciutto
8 thin slices mozzarella cheese
3 tablespoons olive oil
1 small onion, chopped

1 clove garlic, minced
1 16-ounce can Italian-style
  peeled tomatoes
½ cup white wine
Salt and pepper
8 thin strips mozzarella cheese
Parsley sprigs

Pound the meat with a mallet to ⅛ inch thickness. Sprinkle with salt, pepper and a little sage. Cut into 8 rectangular pieces. Cut the slices of prosciutto in half. Top the veal pieces with a piece of ham and a slice of mozzarella. Roll jelly-roll fashion and tie with string. In a large skillet, heat the oil and sauté the veal rolls until browned. Remove from the pan. Add the onion and garlic and sauté until tender. Break the tomatoes up with a fork and add to the skillet, with the white wine and salt and pepper. Mix well. Add the veal rolls and cover. Simmer 1½ hours or until tender. Top with the mozzarella strips, cover and melt the cheese.

Serve on a bed of hot cooked spaghetti, topped with the sauce and garnished with the parsley sprigs.

Makes 4 servings.

veal with marsala wine

vitello alla marsala

1 pound thinly sliced leg of
  veal
  or 1 pound tenderized
    unbreaded veal steaks
2 eggs
½ cup flour

Salt and pepper
5 tablespoons butter (divided)
1 cup thinly sliced fresh
  mushrooms
⅓ cup marsala wine
⅔ cup beef broth

Lightly pound the leg of veal (if used) to an even thickness. Beat the eggs well in a shallow pie plate. Place the meat in the egg mixture and let stand 30 minutes, turning occasionally. Combine the flour and salt and pepper to taste. Drain the veal and dredge in the flour mixture. Heat 3 tablespoons of the butter in a heavy skillet over medium heat until hot and foamy. Add the veal and sauté, turning, until golden brown. Remove the veal from the pan and keep warm on a platter. Melt the remaining 2 tablespoons of butter in the skillet and sauté the mushrooms until tender. Add the wine and beef broth and cook 5 minutes. Pour over the veal and serve.

Makes 4 servings.

calves liver — milanese

veal scallopini in lemon sauce
scaloppine al limone

1¼ pounds veal for scallopini
2½ tablespoons flour
Salt
White pepper
6 tablespoons clarified butter
¼ cup chicken broth
¼ cup white wine
½ of a fresh lemon, thinly sliced
1 tablespoon finely chopped parsley

Arrange the veal slices close together on a cutting board or waxed paper and lightly sprinkle with the flour, salt and white pepper. Turn and flour and season the other side of the meat. Heat the clarified butter in a large heavy skillet. Quickly brown the veal a few pieces at a time on both sides.

Remove from the pan and keep warm. Add the chicken broth, wine, and lemon slices. Push the lemon slices down into the liquid. Reduce the heat to simmer, cover the pan and cook over low heat for 5 minutes. Place the veal on a heated platter, pour the sauce over the meat and sprinkle with the parsley.

Makes 4 servings.

calves liver and onions
fegato alla veneziana

2 medium onions, thinly sliced
2 tablespoons olive oil
1 tablespoon butter
¼ teaspoon ground sage
2 tablespoons dry white wine
  or 1 tablespoon lemon juice
1 pound calves liver, sliced
  ½ inch thick
½ cup all-purpose flour
Salt and pepper
¼ cup cooking oil
1 tablespoon chopped fresh parsley

Sauté the onions in the olive oil and butter until soft and lightly browned. Add the sage and wine. Cover and reduce the heat to low. Simmer while cooking the liver. Take the calves liver slices and cut into ¾-inch-wide strips, 3 to 4 inches long. Drain well. Combine the flour, salt and pepper on a plate. Heat the oil over moderate heat in a heavy skillet. Dredge the liver, shaking off the excess, and fry until lightly browned. Drain and keep warm while cooking the remaining liver. Place the liver in a serving dish, top with the onion mixture and sprinkle with the parsley. Serve with risotto or polenta.

Makes 4 servings.

cauliflower with tomato sauce

calves liver— milanese

fegatelli alla milanese

1 pound calves liver, unsliced
  if possible
¼ cup olive oil
2 tablespoons butter
½ pound sliced fresh
  mushrooms
½ cup slivered Genoa salami
1 medium onion, peeled and
  chopped

4 medium tomatoes, peeled
  and quartered
½ cup dry white wine
¾ teaspoon dried sweet basil,
  crumbled
Salt and pepper, to taste

Cut the calves liver into ¾-inch cubes (partially freeze the liver for easy slicing) and drain in a colander for 15 to 20 minutes. If a whole piece of calves liver is not available, cut the sliced liver into thin strips and drain. In a heavy skillet heat 2 tablespoons oil and 1 tablespoon butter over moderate heat. Add the mushrooms, salami and onions and sauté until the onions are tender. Remove with a slotted spoon and reserve. Add the remaining butter and oil to the skillet and heat. Add the liver and sauté until lightly browned. Add the tomatoes, wine, seasoning and reserved ingredients. Stir well. Cover and simmer over low heat 10 to 15 minutes. Serve with risotto or cooked macaroni.

Makes 4 servings.

lamb chops — venetian-style

vegetables

asparagus— milanese style
spargi alla milanese

1 10-ounce package frozen asparagus spears, partially thawed
1 tablespoon melted butter or margarine (divided)
2 tablespoons dry sherry
½ teaspoon seasoned salt and pepper mixture
⅓ cup Italian-style bread crumbs
2 tablespoons grated Romano cheese

Preheat the oven to 350°F. Separate the asparagus spears and place in a 9-inch pie plate. Mix the melted butter or margarine, sherry, and salt and pepper mixture and pour over the asparagus. Tightly cover with foil and bake for 30 minutes or until crisp-tender. Uncover and drain the liquid from the asparagus. Melt the remaining butter and combine with the crumbs. Sprinkle over the asparagus. Sprinkle with the cheese. Broil until the crumbs are lightly browned and the cheese is melted.

Makes 3 servings.

romano beans in tomato sauce
fagiolini con salsa pomodori

2 tablespoons olive oil
1 small garlic clove, minced
2 tablespoons chopped onion
¼ cup minced prosciutto or
  baked ham
½ cup tomato sauce
Salt and pepper
2 tablespoons water
1 9-ounce package frozen
  Italian (or Romano) green
  beans

Heat the oil in a medium saucepan. Add the garlic, onion and prosciutto and sauté for 5 minutes. Add the tomato sauce, salt, and pepper, and water and mix well. Add the frozen green beans and bring to a boil, stirring to break up the beans. Cover, reduce the heat to low and cook 15 minutes.

Makes 3 to 4 servings.

roman-style green beans
fagiolini alla romana

1 9-ounce package frozen
  French-cut green beans
1 tablespoon fresh lemon juice
2 tablespoons olive oil
¼ teaspoon dried oregano,
  crumbled
⅛ teaspoon garlic powder
Salt and pepper
¼ cup sliced black olives

Cook the beans in boiling salted water according to the package directions. Drain well. Meanwhile, combine the lemon juice, olive oil, seasonings and olives in a small saucepan and heat through. Pour over the cooked beans and toss well. Serve immediately.

Makes 4 servings.

mixed vegetables in the italian manner
vegetali misto

2 tablespoons olive oil
1 medium onion, peeled and
  chopped
1 clove garlic, peeled and
  minced
1 green pepper, cleaned and
  cut into chunks
1 red pepper, cleaned and cut
  into chunks
½ pound eggplant (1 small or
  ½ of a large eggplant),
  unpeeled and cut into
  chunks
1 medium zucchini, cut into ½-
  inch slices
3 medium tomatoes, peeled
  and quartered
¼ teaspoon dried rosemary,
  crumbled
¼ teaspoon dried basil,
  crumbled
Salt and pepper

Heat the olive oil in a large skillet. Add the onion and garlic and sauté until the onion and garlic are transparent. Add the peppers, eggplant, zucchini, tomatoes and seasonings and bring to a boil. Reduce the heat to low and cook until the vegetables are tender.

Makes 3 to 4 servings.

carrots piedmontese
carote alla piedmontese

3 cups peeled carrots, thinly sliced
2 tablespoons butter or margarine
¼ cup onion, finely chopped
1 small clove garlic, peeled
½ teaspoon salt
2 teaspoons red wine vinegar
2 teaspoons freeze-dried chopped chives

Cook the carrots in boiling salted water in a medium, covered saucepan for 5 minutes. Drain in a colander. Melt the butter in the saucepan. Add the onion, garlic, salt and drained carrots. Stir well. Cover and cook over low heat 10 minutes or until the carrots are crisp but tender. Remove and discard the garlic clove. Stir in the vinegar and chives and let stand several minutes, then serve.

Makes 4 servings.

sautéed broccoli
broccoli sauté

1 pound fresh young broccoli
Boiling salted water
3 tablespoons olive oil
1 clove garlic, peeled and chopped
Salt and pepper, to taste

Cut off any dry woody stems and trim the broccoli of all discolored parts and dead leaves. Separate into small spears and peel the stalks with a vegetable peeler. Cook in 1 inch of boiling salted water until crisp but tender. Drain well. In a large skillet, heat the oil over moderate heat. Sauté the garlic until lightly browned. Add the broccoli and sauté, stirring constantly for 5 minutes. Add salt and pepper to taste and serve topped with the oil from the pan.

Makes 4 servings.

zucchini and potatoes
zucchini e patate

4 medium potatoes
Boiling salted water
2 medium zucchini squash
¼ cup olive oil
½ teaspoon garlic salt
¼ teaspoon pepper

Peel the potatoes and dice. Cook in boiling salted water until tender. Drain well and keep warm. Meanwhile, cut the ends from the zucchini, wash well and slice ½ inch thick. Pat dry on paper towels. In a large skillet, heat the oil over moderate heat. Cook the zucchini, stirring occasionally until crisp but tender. Add the zucchini, oil, and seasonings to the potatoes and continue to cook over low heat for 5 to 10 minutes, crushing the potatoes slightly until the mixture becomes thick. Serve hot.

Makes 4 servings.

zucchini with tomato sauce
zucchini con salsa di pomodoro

2 medium zucchini squash
3 tablespoons olive oil
1 8-ounce can tomato sauce
½ teaspoon dried oregano, crumbled
Salt and pepper

Trim the blossom end from the zucchini and scrub well under running water. Leave the skin intact (do not peel), and slice in ½-inch thick slices. Dry on paper towels. Heat the oil in a large saucepan over medium heat. Sauté the zucchini in the oil, stirring, for approximately 10 minutes or until crisp but tender. Add the tomato sauce and seasonings and reduce the heat to simmer. Cook 10 more minutes. Serve hot.

Makes 4 servings.

mushrooms with garlic and oil

funghi aglio e olio

1 pound fresh mushrooms
2 tablespoons olive oil
2 cloves garlic
¼ teaspoon salt

Clean the mushrooms with a damp cloth or, if necessary, wash in cold water. Remove the steams and reserve for another use. Pat dry, Cut large mushrooms in quarters. Cut medium-sized mushrooms in half and leave the small ones whole.

Heat the oil over moderate heat in a heavy skillet. Peel the garlic cloves and slice. Sauté the garlic in the oil until lightly browned. Remove the garlic from the pan with a slotted spoon. Sprinkle the oil with the salt. Add the mushrooms and sauté over moderately high heat until the liquid coming from the mushrooms has evaporated. Stir constantly to prevent sticking. Reduce the heat to low and cook uncovered for 40 minutes, stirring occasionally, until the mushrooms are golden. Serve with steak or other meat dishes.

Makes 4 servings.

fried mushrooms

funghi fritto

Excellent on a hot antipasto tray or with steak!!

3 dozen mushrooms, about 1 inch in diameter
2 eggs
1 tablespoon water
½ teaspoon salt
¼ teaspoon pepper
½ cup flour
1 cup Italian-style bread crumbs
Oil for frying

Wash, trim the stems, and drain the mushrooms. Beat the egg, water, salt and pepper together. Impale on a fork and dip in flour, then dip in the egg mixture and coat with bread crumbs. Allow to dry while heating 3 inches of vegetable oil to 360°F in a deep-fat fryer or deep saucepan. Fry a few at a time for 4 minutes or until golden brown. Drain and serve hot.

Makes 6 servings.

macaroni with cauliflower

penne con cauliflore

1 (10-ounce) package frozen cauliflower
3 cups dry uncooked penne, rigatoni or ziti (or the macaroni of your choice)
2 tablespoons butter
2 tablespoons olive oil
1 clove garlic, peeled and minced
¼ teaspoon dried oregano, crumbled
½ tablespoon dehydrated parsley flakes
Salt and pepper
Grated Parmesan cheese

Cook the cauliflower in boiling salted water until crisp but tender. Drain well. Meanwhile, cook the macaroni in boiling salted water, according to the package directions. Drain and rinse briefly with cool water. In a large skillet, heat the butter and oil over moderate heat. Add the garlic and sauté 2 minutes. Add the cauliflower and sauté for 5 minutes or until lightly browned. Add the macaroni, oregano, parsley and salt and pepper and heat through. Serve sprinkled with the Parmesan cheese.

Makes 4 servings.

cauliflower with tomato sauce

caulifiore e salsa pomodori

1 medium-sized head of cauliflower, trimmed of the outer green leaves
6 cups water
2 teaspoons salt

sauce
3 tablespoons olive oil
2 chopped shallots *or* ¼ cup chopped onion
¼ cup ham, finely chopped
¼ cup canned sliced mushrooms
1½ tablespoons flour
2 tablespoons tomato paste
¾ cup hot chicken broth
¼ cup white wine
¼ cup chopped parsley
Salt and pepper, to taste

Make a deep x-shaped cut in the base of the cauliflower, then place on a vegetable steamer rack. Combine the water and salt in a large heavy kettle and bring to a boil. Lower the rack into the kettle, cover the pot tightly and cook 20 minutes. The cauliflower should be crisp but tender. Drain.

Meanwhile, heat the oil in a saucepan. Sauté the shallots or onion in oil until lightly browned. Add the ham and mushrooms and sauté 2 minutes. Remove the onion, ham, and mushrooms with a slotted spoon. Add the flour to the oil in the saucepan and cook until bubbly. Combine the chicken broth and tomato paste and add to the saucepan, stirring well. Add the wine, reserved ingredients, parsley, salt and pepper and serve hot over the cauliflower.

Makes 6 servings.

fried eggplant

melenzana fritta

1 medium eggplant (about 1 pound)
1 egg
2 tablespoons water
⅓ cup flour
¾ cup dry bread crumbs
2 tablespoons grated Parmesan cheese
Cooking oil

Peel the eggplant and cut into ½-inch-thick slices. Soak in cold salted water to cover for 15 minutes. Meanwhile, beat the egg with the water in a shallow pan. Place the flour on a sheet of waxed paper. On a separate sheet of waxed paper, combine the bread crumbs and Parmesan cheese.

Drain the eggplant well and pat dry with paper towels. Dip in the flour, then in the egg mixture, and finally coat well with bread crumbs, shaking off the excess. Place on a baking sheet until all the slices are coated. Heat ½ inch of vegetable oil in a large heavy skillet over moderate heat. Cook a few slices of eggplant at a time until golden, turning once. Drain on paper towels and serve immediately.

Makes 4 servings.

Variation: 2 medium zucchini squash can be substituted for the eggplant. Trim the ends from the zucchini and cut in half crosswise. Then cut the unpeeled zucchini into sticks. Do not soak in cold water. Bread in the same manner as the eggplant and fry until golden. Drain on paper towels and serve.

breads: sweet and savory

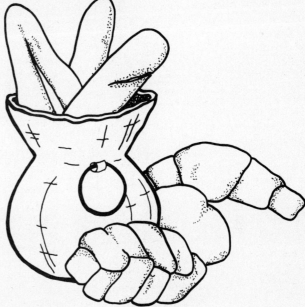

crisp italian bread
pane italiano

1 package active dry yeast
⅓ cup warm water
3½ to 4 cups all-purpose flour
2 teaspoons salt

1¼ cups water
1 tablespoon coarse cornmeal
1 egg white
1 tablespoon cold water

Dissolve the yeast in the ⅓ cup of warm water (105 to 115°F). Mix well and let stand 5 minutes. Mix the flour and salt together. In a large bowl, combine the dissolved yeast and add the 1¼ cups water. Slowly add the flour mixture, stirring well after each addition, to form a stiff dough. Turn out on a floured board and knead for 10 to 15 minutes, adding flour as necessary, until smooth and elastic. Place in a greased bowl and rotate to coat the surface of the dough. Cover and let rise in a warm place 1 to 2 hours or until double in bulk. Punch down. Lightly flour a smooth surface. Toss the dough with the flour until no longer sticky. Divide into two parts. Roll the dough with a rolling pin to a 12 × 8-inch rectangle. Roll up jelly-roll fashion, beginning with a 12-inch side to form a long loaf. Pinch the edges to seal. Taper the ends of the loaf by rolling between the palms of the hands. Sprinkle a large baking sheet with cornmeal. Place the two loaves on the baking sheet and cover with a towel. Let rise in a warm place until double in bulk (1 to 2 hours). With a razor blade, make 3 diagonal slits in the surface of the loaf. Beat the egg white and water together until well-mixed. Brush the loaves with the mixture. Preheat the oven to 400°F. Put the bread on the middle shelf of the oven and place a small cake pan with 1 inch of hot water on the shelf beneath it. Bake for 15 minutes, then reduce the heat to 350°F and bake for an additional 15 minutes. The loaves should sound hollow when tapped and be well-browned. Cool on a rack.

Makes 2 12-inch loaves.

bread sticks
grissini

1 recipe Crisp Italian Bread
  (see Index)
1 egg white
1 tablespoon cold water
3 tablespoons sesame seeds

Prepare the Italian bread dough and allow to rise once as directed in the recipe. Punch the dough down. Lightly flour a smooth surface. Toss the dough on the floured surface until no longer sticky. Divide the dough into 24 equal parts. Roll the pieces of dough into 10-inch-long sticks. Place on baking sheets 1 inch apart. Cover with towels and allow to rise in a warm place until double in bulk (about 45 minutes). Preheat the oven to 425°F. Meanwhile, beat the egg white and water together. Brush the bread sticks well with the egg white mixture and sprinkle with the sesame seeds. Place the baking sheet or sheets (you will have to bake only one or two sheets at a time, keeping the remainder covered) on the middle shelf in the oven. Place a cake pan with 1 inch of hot water in it on the shelf below the bread sticks. Bake for 10 minutes at 425°F and then reduce the heat to 350°F for 15 to 20 minutes or until browned and dry throughout. Cool on a rack.

Makes 24.

Note: The process of rolling each piece of dough to form a 10-inch stick is very time-consuming, so it is wise to have help or allow a leisurely afternoon for this project. As each baking sheet is filled with bread sticks, cover it and put in a warm place to rise. In this way, all the bread sticks will not be ready to bake at the same time.

batter bread—italian-style
panne con pepperoni

This loaf is delicious served with soup and salad or try it buttered and grilled with mozzarella cheese!!

1 package active dry yeast
1¼ cups warm water
  (105 to 115°F)
2 tablespoons vegetable oil
1 tablespoon sugar
1 teaspoon salt
¼ teaspoon garlic powder
½ teaspoon dried oregano,
  crumbled
3 cups all-purpose flour
  (divided)
¼ cup finely diced pepperoni

In a large mixing bowl, dissolve the yeast in the warm water. Add the oil, sugar, salt, garlic powder and oregano and 2 cups of flour. Using an electric mixer, combine the ingredients on low speed. Then, increase the speed to medium and beat for 3 minutes, scraping the bowl occasionally. Stir in the remaining flour and the pepperoni. Scrape the batter down from the sides of the bowl. Cover and let rise in a warm place (80°F) until double in bulk (45 to 60 minutes). Stir the batter down and spread evenly in a greased 9 × 5 × 3-inch loaf pan. Cover and let rise until double (30 to 40 minutes). Preheat the oven to 375°F and bake for 35 to 40 minutes or until the loaf sounds hollow when tapped. Cool on a rack before slicing.

Makes 1 9 × 5-inch loaf.

pizza

Feel free to use the toppings of your choice on this delicious crust!

crust

1½ cups all-purpose flour
½ teaspoon salt
1 package active dry yeast

½ cup warm water
  (105 to 115°F)
1 tablespoon vegetable oil

sauce

1 tablespoon olive oil
¼ cup onion, finely chopped
1 clove garlic, minced
1 16-ounce can Italian style
  peeled tomatoes

2 tablespoons tomato paste
½ teaspoon dried oregano,
  crumbled
½ teaspoon sugar
½ teaspoon salt

topping

½ pound bulk sausage
1 cup shredded mozzarella
  cheese

¼ cup grated Parmesan
  cheese
1 4-ounce can sliced
  mushrooms, drained

To make the crust, combine the flour and salt and set aside. Dissolve the yeast in the warm water. Add the oil. Stir in the flour and salt. Turn out on a lightly floured board and knead until smooth and elastic. Lightly grease a medium bowl. Place the dough in the bowl and rotate to grease the whole surface. Cover the bowl and place in a warm place until double in bulk (1 to 1½ hours).

Meanwhile, make the sauce. In a medium saucepan, heat the oil. Add the onion and garlic and sauté over medium heat for 5 minutes, stirring constantly. Do not brown. Puree the tomatoes and their juice in an electric blender or break up with a fork. Add the tomatoes, tomato paste, and seasonings to the saucepan. Bring the mixture to a boil, then reduce the heat to low. Cook, uncovered, stirring occasionally for 50 minutes, or until thick. Set aside to cool.

When the dough has doubled in bulk, punch down. Place the dough on a lightly floured surface and let rest 10 minutes. Roll to a 12-inch circle and place in a 12-inch-round pizza pan. Preheat the oven to 400°F and bake the crust for 13 to 15 minutes. Meanwhile, lightly fry the sausage. Remove the crust from the oven and top with the sauce. Sprinkle with the mozzarella and Parmesan cheese. Top with the sausage and mushrooms. Return to the oven and bake for 10 more minutes. Remove from the pan and cut.

Makes 1 12-inch pizza.

Note: The sauce recipe can be easily doubled and frozen for later use.

pizza

calzone

calzone all 'italiana

(literally translated this means trouser legs)

crust

2½ cups all-purpose flour
1 teaspoon salt
1 package active dry yeast
1 cup warm water
2 tablespoons cooking oil

or

Substitute 1 package hot roll mix prepared according to the package directions

filling

2 tablespoons olive oil
1 medium onion, chopped
1 clove garlic, peeled and
  minced
½ cup fresh mushrooms,
  chopped
½ cup chopped prosciutto
½ cup chopped salami
¾ cup shredded mozzarella
  cheese
2 tablespoons chopped parsley
½ teaspoon dried sweet basil,
  crumbled
Salt and pepper
1 egg yolk

glaze

1 egg
1 tablespoon water

Stir the flour and salt together and set aside. Dissolve the yeast in the warm water. Add the oil. Stir in the flour mixture. Turn out on a lightly floured board and knead until smooth and elastic. Lightly grease a medium bowl. Place the dough in the bowl and rotate to grease the surface. Cover and let rise in a warm place until double in bulk. (Approximately 2 hours)

Meanwhile, make the filling. Heat the oil in a medium skillet. Add the onion, garlic and mushrooms and sauté 5 minutes. Remove from the heat and allow to cool. Add the remaining filling ingredients and mix well. Set aside.

Lightly flour a smooth surface. Punch the dough down, and toss the dough on the floured surface until it is no longer sticky. Divide the dough into 12 equal parts. Roll each part to a 5-inch circle. Spoon about 2 tablespoons of the filling on ½ of the round. Fold over and moisten the edge lightly with water. Seal by pressing with the fingers. Place on lightly greased cookie sheets. Beat the egg and water together and brush the turnovers thoroughly with the mixture. Bake in a preheated 375°F oven for 20 minutes or until golden and serve hot.

Calzone may also be deep fried at 360°F (*do not* brush with the egg and water mixture) until golden.

Makes 12 turnovers (about 6 servings).

Variation: For another tasty filling, combine 8 ounces shredded mozzarella cheese, ½ cup drained and chopped canned tomatoes, and ½ teaspoon dried sweet basil, crumbled.

calzone

herb and cheese bread ring

This bread makes a delicious accompaniment to any antipasto.

1 13¾-ounce package hot-roll mix
¾ cup warm water (105 to 115°F)
1 egg, lightly beaten
1 teaspoon dried oregano, crumbled
1 teaspoon dried sweet basil, crumbled
Flour

1 cup coarsely shredded sharp cheddar cheese
1 tablespoon dried parsley flakes
1 egg yolk
1 tablespoon milk
3 tablespoons grated Parmesan cheese
Paprika

In a large mixing bowl, dissolve the yeast from the hot-roll mix. Add the egg and mix. Stir in the flour from the roll mix and the oregano and sweet basil. Stir well to incorporate all the flour. Cover with a towel and let stand in a warm place until double in bulk (about 45 minutes). Punch down. Flour a smooth surface and turn out the dough. Knead lightly until no longer sticky. Roll the dough with a rolling pin to a rectangle 8 × 18 inches. Sprinkle evenly with the cheddar cheese and sprinkle with the parsley flakes. Roll like a jelly roll, beginning on an 18-inch edge. Pinch the edges to seal. Form into a ring and pinch to seal. Place on a slightly greased cookie sheet. With a very sharp knife, slit the outside edge of the ring at 2-inch intervals. Cover with a towel and let rinse in a warm place until double in bulk. Beat the egg yolk and milk together. Brush the ring well with the egg-yolk mixture. Sprinkle with the Parmesan cheese and dust with paprika. Bake in a preheated 350°F oven for 30 to 35 minutes or until golden and the loaf sounds hollow when tapped. Remove from the cookie sheet and cool on a rack.

Makes 1 large loaf (serves about 6).

honey balls
strufoli

2½ cups all-purpose flour
½ teaspoon baking powder
4 eggs
1 tablespoon cooking oil
Vegetable oil for frying

honey syrup
¾ cup honey
⅓ cup sugar
⅓ cup water
1 tablespoon lemon juice
Multicolored candy decorettes

Sift the flour and baking powder together. Make a well in the center of the flour mixture. Beat the eggs and oil together and pour into the well. Stir with a fork to form a soft dough that can be handled. Turn out on a lightly floured board and knead until smooth and elastic. Divide the dough into 10 equal pieces and cover with a towel. Roll the pieces, one at a time, into an 18-inch-long string and cut into 36 small pieces. Place on a lightly floured cookied sheet. Heat 3 inches of vegetable oil in a heavy saucepan to 375°F on a deep-fry thermometer. Fry a few at a time until golden brown and remove with a slotted spoon. Drain on paper towels.

Next make the syrup. In a heavy saucepan, combine the honey, sugar, water and lemon juice. Cook, stirring constantly, over moderate heat until the sugar dissolves. Continue cooking over low heat, uncovered, 15 minutes without stirring until thickened. Add the fried pastry and stir to coat. Pile the honey-coated pastry on a platter in a cone shape. Sprinkle with decorettes.

Makes about 4 cups.

raised doughnuts
zeppole (also called pizza fritta)

4 cups all-purpose flour
¼ teaspoon salt
1 cup warm water (105 to 115°F)
1 package active dry yeast
5 tablespoons granulated sugar
1 egg, lightly beaten (room temperature)
Vegetable oil for frying
Confectioners' sugar

Sift together the flour and salt and place in a medium-sized mixing bowl and set aside. Dissolve the yeast in the warm water. Let stand 5 minutes. Stir in the sugar and egg, mixing well. Make a well in the center of the flour mixture and add the yeast mixture. Mix thoroughly with a fork to moisten all the flour mixture. Turn the dough out on a lightly floured board and knead for 20 minutes or until the dough is smooth and elastic. Place the dough in a greased bowl, cover with a towel, and leave in a warm place to rise until double in bulk (1 to 2 hours). Place 4 inches of oil in a deep-fat fryer or 2 inches of oil in a heavy skillet and begin heating. Lightly oil your hands. Take a golf-ball-sized piece of the dough between the palms and form into a square (2 × 2½ inches). Punch several holes in the dough with your finger. Drop the dough immediately into 365°F fat and fry until golden. Drain on absorbent paper. Sprinkle with confectioners' sugar and serve. Keep any leftovers in a plastic bag and reheat on a cookie sheet in a warm oven.

Makes about 30.

holiday coffee bread
pannetone

2 packages active dry yeast
½ cup lukewarm water (105 to 115°F)
½ cup sugar
3 eggs
½ teaspoon anise extract
½ teaspoon salt
½ cup butter, softened
3 cups flour (approximately)
½ cup citron, diced
½ cup dark or golden raisins
1 tablespoon flour
2 tablespoons butter or margarine, melted

Mix the yeast, water and 2 teaspoons of the sugar in a small bowl, stirring well. Cover and let stand 3 to 5 minutes or until bubbly and double in volume. In a large bowl, combine the eggs, remaining sugar, anise and salt and add the yeast mixture. Beat by hand or with an electric mixer for 2 minutes. Add the butter and 1½ cups of the flour and beat to combine. Add ½ cup more flour and beat in by hand. Turn out on a lightly floured board and knead in enough flour to make a soft dough that is no longer sticky. Form into a ball, place in a greased bowl, cover and let rise in a warm place until double in bulk.

Lightly coat the citron and raisins with the tablespoon of flour. Punch the dough down, turn out on a floured surface and gently knead the fruit into the dough. Lightly grease a 1½-quart soufflé dish and place the dough in the dish or form into a ball and place on a greased baking sheet. Cover and let rise until double in bulk. Brush with melted butter or margarine. Preheat the oven to 400°F and bake for 10 minutes. Reduce the heat to 350°F and bake for 30 to 40 minutes more, brushing once with butter, until crisp and golden.

Turn out on a rack and cool. Let stand 24 hours before slicing. Makes 1 loaf that serves 8.

sweets

italian sesame sticks
biscotti regina

These cookies are crispy "dunkers" and are excellent served with espresso or red wine.

1 cup butter or margarine
1½ cups sugar
1 teaspoon vanilla
3 eggs
5 cups self-rising flour
Milk
About 2 cups white sesame
    seeds

Cream the butter with an electric mixer until light. Gradually add the sugar, beating well. Add the vanilla and the eggs, one at a time, and beat well after each addition. Sift the self-rising flour and add to the creamed mixture, mixing just until smooth. Cover the dough and refrigerate for several hours or overnight. Pour 1 inch of milk into a shallow pie pan. Sprinkle the sesame seed on a large sheet of waxed paper. Using a scant tablespoon of the dough roll on a board or between the palms of the hands to a 3½-inch-long log. Dip in the milk and then roll in the sesame seeds to coat well. Place on a greased cookie sheet 1 inch apart. Bake in a preheated 375°F oven for 15 minutes. Cool on a rack.
Makes 6 dozen.

Note: Any leftover seeds can be dried and toasted in the oven and sprinkled on breads or salads.

del's sicilian iced cookies
bicotti alla siciliana

dough

½ cup margarine
½ cup hydrogenated shortening
½ cup sugar
2 eggs
1 teaspoon vanilla
2 cups all-purpose flour
2 teaspoons baking powder
6 tablespoons milk

icing

2¼ cups sifted confectioners' sugar
3 tablespoons maraschino cherry liqueur
A few drops red food coloring
2 tablespoons warm water
Colored candy decorettes

Melt the margarine and shortening in a medium saucepan. Remove from the heat and add the sugar. Mix well. Beat the eggs well and add to the mixture. Add the vanilla and mix well. Combine the flour and baking powder. Add to the butter and sugar mixture and stir well. Slowly add the milk and mix to form a stiff dough. Refrigerate the dough several hours or overnight. Drop the mixture by rounded teaspoons onto a greased cookie sheet. Bake at 350°F for 8 to 10 minutes or until lightly browned. Cool on a rack.

When the cookies have cooled completely, make the icing. Place the confectioners' sugar in a small mixing bowl. Make a well in the center. Place the cherry liqueur and the food coloring in the well (use enough to make the frosting a pale pink). Stir the sugar into the liquid to form a very stiff paste. Slowly add the warm water, while stirring, until the mixture is smooth and spreadable. Ice the tops of the cookies and sprinkle with the candy decorettes. Allow to dry on the cake racks. Store in an airtight container.

Makes 4 dozen cookies.

florentines

½ cup butter
¾ cup sugar
3 eggs
¾ teaspoon almond extract
1 teaspoon grated orange peel
2½ cups all-purpose flour

1½ teaspoons baking powder
¼ teaspoon salt
1 cup ground almonds
1 cup semisweet chocolate chips
2 tablespoons hot water

Cream the butter and sugar. Add the eggs one at a time, beating well after each addition. Beat in the almond extract and the orange peel. Sift together the flour, baking powder, and salt and add to the creamed mixture and stir well to combine. Add the almonds and stir well. Refrigerate the dough for several hours. Lightly grease a cookie sheet. Form the dough into loaves 1½ inches wide and ½ inch thick. Make sure the loaves are several inches apart as the cookies spread in baking. Make the loaves as long as your cookie sheet allows, but leave at least an inch space between the end of the loaf and the edge of the cookie sheet to prevent burning. Bake at 375°F for 12 to 15 minutes or until lightly browned and a toothpick inserted in the center of the loaf comes out clean. While still warm, cut the loaves into ¾-inch strips and cool on a cake rack.

Melt the chocolate chips over hot water, stirring occasionally. When completely melted, stir in just enough boiling water to make a thick mixture with consistency of layer-cake icing. Dip both ends of the cookie strips in the chocolate and allow to dry on a rack until the chocolate has hardened.

Makes 3½ to 4 dozen cookies

florentines

cannoli

neopolitan torte

sicilian
cheese-filled
pastries
cannoli

pastry

2 cups flour
1 teaspoon salt
2 tablespoons sugar
2 tablespoons soft butter, cut
  into small pieces
1 egg, beaten
10 tablespoons white wine
Oil for frying
5-inch long x 1-inch in
  diameter cannoli forms or
  pieces of dowel

filling

⅔ cup sugar
½ cup flour
⅛ teaspoon salt
2 cups scalded milk
2 eggs, lightly beaten
½ teaspoon vanilla extract
¼ teaspoon almond extract
1 pound ricotta cheese
½ cup powdered sugar
½ cup finely chopped candied
  fruit
1 1-ounce block semisweet
  chocolate, grated

Combine the flour and salt in a mixing bowl. Make a well in the center and add the sugar, butter and egg. Add the wine and stir with a fork until the liquid is absorbed. Turn out on a floured board and knead until smooth. Divide the dough into four equal parts. Roll out on a floured surface until 1/16th of an inch thick. Cut into 3½ inch squares. Roll the squares diagonally onto the forms, overlapping the corners. Seal with a little water. Heat ¾ of an inch of oil in a heavy skillet to 375°F. Fry the cannolis, 3 at a time, in the hot oil. When light golden, remove from the oil and slip off of the forms as soon as they are cool enough to handle. Allow to cool completely.

Next make the cream filling. Combine the sugar, flour and salt in the top of a double boiler. Slowly stir in the scalded milk. Cook the mixture over boiling water until the mixture thickens. Combine 1 cup of the custard mixture with the eggs and beat well. Pour the mixture back into the double boiler and continue to cook, stirring, 3 minutes. Cool, then stir in the flavoring (filling must be cold before adding the ricotta). Beat the ricotta and powdered sugar until the ricotta is smooth. Fold in the custard, mixed fruit and chocolate.

Fill the cannoli with a small spatula, carefully packing the filling. Refrigerate until serving time.

Makes 30 to 35.

Note: Shells can be made ahead and frozen and filled as needed.

almond
dessert
biscuit tortoni

1 cup milk
2 eggs, separated
½ cup sugar
½ tablespoon unflavored
  gelatin
2 tablespoons milk

1 cup heavy cream
8 crushed almond macaroons
½ teaspoon almond extract
Almond macaroon crumbs
Candied cherries

In a medium saucepan, scald the milk. Cool slightly. Beat the egg yolks and sugar together until well-blended. Pour a little of the milk into the egg-yolk mixture. Beat well and add to the scalded milk in the saucepan. Cook over moderate heat, stirring constantly, until the mixture coats a spoon. Soften the gelatin in the 2 tablespoons of milk. Dissolve the gelatin in the hot custard. Stir well. Strain and cool the mixture covered with waxed paper. Beat the egg whites until stiff and fold into the custard. Whip the cream until stiff and fold the cream, macaroons and flavoring into the custard. Place in 8 individual serving dishes and garnish with macaroon crumbs and candied cherries. Refrigerate until ready to serve.

Makes 8 servings.

italian chocolate cookies
gocci di cioccolata

dough

4 cups all-purpose flour
1 teaspoon baking powder
¼ cup cocoa
¾ teaspoon ground cinnamon
¾ teaspoon ground allspice
¾ teaspoon ground cloves
¾ teaspoon ground nutmeg

¾ cup raisins
¾ cup chopped walnuts
1¼ cups hydrogenated shortening
1 cup plus 2 tablespoons sugar
2 eggs, slightly beaten
1 cup milk

frosting

3 cups confectioners' sugar
4 tablespoons milk
1½ teaspoons rum flavoring

Several drops red food coloring

Sift the flour. Add the baking powder, cocoa, and spices to the flour and sift 2 more times. Add the raisins and walnuts to the flour mixture and mix well.

Cream the shortening and sugar until light. Add the eggs and beat well. Add the flour a little at a time alternately with the milk until all the ingredients are combined. Mix well. Refrigerate the dough for several hours or overnight. Using a rounded teaspoon of dough, form into small balls. Place on a lightly greased cookie sheet 1 inch apart. Bake at 400°F for 10 minutes or until a toothpick inserted in the center of a cookie comes out clean. Remove from the cookie sheet and cool on a cake rack.

When the cookies have cooled completely, make the frosting. Combine the confectioners' sugar, milk, flavoring and food coloring and mix well. Spread the top of each cookie with 1 teaspoon of icing and allow to dry on waxed paper. Store in airtight cookie tins.
Makes about 8 dozen.

neopolitan torte
torta alla napoletana

dough

¾ cup butter
1 cup sugar
2 eggs
½ cup ground almonds
1½ teaspoons grated lemon rind
3½ cups flour

filling

1⅓ cups raspberry jam (very thick, with lots of fruit)

glaze and garnish

2 cups sifted confectioners' sugar
2 tablespoons hot water
2 tablespoons maraschino cherry liqueur
A few drops red food coloring
½ cup whipping cream
6 candied cherries, halved

Cream the butter and sugar well. Beat in the eggs one at a time. Add the almonds and lemon rind and mix. Slowly add the flour, mixing in well by hand. Form into a large ball, cover, and refrigerate 1 hour.

Divide the dough into 5 equal parts. Grease the bottom of a 10-inch springform pan. Roll out the dough 1 part at a time and cut to fit the springform pan. Place one layer of dough on the bottom section of the springform pan. Spread with ⅓ cup of the jam. Top with another layer of dough, spread with jam, and proceed as above until all the dough is used. Place the ring around the springform pan. Bake at 400°F on the bottom oven rack for 45 minutes. Cool and place on a platter.

Mix the confectioners' sugar, hot water, and maraschino liqueur and red food coloring to form a smooth glaze. Smooth over the top of the cake. Whip the cream until stiff. Place in a pastry bag fitted with a rose tip and pipe 12 rosettes around the edge of the cake. Top each rosette with ½ of a candied cherry.
Makes 12 servings.

77

frozen ice-cream bombe

frozen ice-cream bombe

cassata di gelati

1½ quarts vanilla ice cream, softened
1 quart raspberry sherbert, softened
¾ quart pistachio ice cream, softened
½ cup diced candied fruit

2 tablespoons rum
3 large egg whites
½ cup sugar
½ cup whipping cream

for garnish
1 cup whipping cream
Candied fruit

Line a 2-quart mold evenly with the vanilla ice cream. Freeze until firm, preferably in a 0°F freezer. Cover the vanilla ice cream evenly with a layer of raspberry sherbert and freeze again. Then cover with a layer of pistachio ice cream and freeze solid.

Cover the chopped candied fruit with the rum and set aside. Beat the egg whites until foamy. Slowly beat in the sugar. Whip the ½ cup of whipping cream until stiff. Fold the cream and rum-soaked fruit into the egg-white meringue, until thoroughly combined. Spoon the egg-white mixture into the center of the molded ice cream. Spread to make a smooth bottom layer. Cover and freeze until firm (5 hours or will keep up to 2 weeks).

To unmold, dip the outside of the mold in hot water for 6 seconds and invert onto a cold platter. Whip the remaining cup of whipping cream until stiff and place in a pastry bag fitted with a decorative tip. Decorate with the cream and candied fruit and serve sliced.

Serves 12 to 16.

78

index

79